GOSPEL FORMED

Living a Grace-Addicted, Truth-Filled, Jesus-Exalting Life

J.A. MEDDERS
FOREWORD BY JARED C. WILSON

Kregel
Publications

Gospel Formed: Living a Grace-Addicted, Truth-Filled, Jesus-Exalting Life
© 2014 by J.A. Medders

Published by Kregel Publications, a division of Kregel, Inc., 2450 Oak Industrial Drive NE, Grand Rapids, MI 49505.

All Scripture quotations, unless otherwise indicated, are from The Holy Bible, English Standard Version® (ESV®), copyright © 2001 by Crossway, a publishing ministry of Good News Publishers. Used by permission. All rights reserved.

Scripture quotations marked NLT are from the Holy Bible, New Living Translation, copyright © 1996, 2004, 2007 by Tyndale House Foundation. Used by permission of Tyndale House Publishers, Inc., Carol Stream, Illinois 60188. All rights reserved.

ISBN 978-0-8254-4358-9

Printed in the United States of America

14 15 16 17 18 / 5 4 3 2 1

"I'm tired of people talking about the gospel as if it were a syllogism on a whiteboard. The gospel ought to give us a dry mouth and hands trembling with joyful exuberance. If the gospel has become something routine to you, not the kind of good news that lights up a Galilean sky with angels, read this book with expectation. J.A. Medders is a pastor, a leader, and, most importantly, a cross-bearing student of a rabbi king who isn't dead anymore. His enthusiasm can shake you out of routine and toward glory."

RUSSELL D. MOORE
President, Ethics & Religious Liberty Commission
Southern Baptist Convention

"The gospel is the message of how all things are made new through Jesus Christ. It is therefore a matter of regret that the theologically minded often talk about this message in ways that are dull and uninspired, not new at all. Thankfully, Jeff Medders doesn't think much of that approach. I commend the fresh approach of *Gospel Formed* to you."

DOUGLAS WILSON
Senior minister, Christ Church
Moscow, Idaho

"Jeff Medders has given us a devotional book that is fresh, biblical, and very funny. "Sola bootstrapa" was not part of my vocabulary before, but it is now. These short readings are words fitly spoken, and they pose grave danger for spiritual weakness. Read this book, savor this gospel, and then get off your couch and take some dominion in the name of Jesus."

OWEN STRACHAN
Author, *Risky Gospel*

"We have become a culture of niches and specialty issues. In all our clamoring for our own soapboxes, we have sidelined the main thing: the gospel. I'm grateful that this book walks our minds and hearts back home to Jesus. Read it to enjoy him!"

JIMMY NEEDHAM
Christian recording artist

For Ivy and Oliver.
Kids, it's all about Jesus. There is no one
more important—more incredible!—than
Jesus. I hope you see the greatest truth in
the universe: God loves sinners like us.

*You are invited to take the comfort of this gospel
truth, that "there is forgiveness with God."*

JOHN OWEN

CONTENTS

FOREWORD

What do Christians today need in order to walk with encouragement through the life events they experience? Is it a newer model of worship? A new set of instructions? The latest innovation in religious technology? A handbook of tips and skills and troubleshooting flowcharts? Do we need more inspirational pick-me-ups? Do Christians need more classes, more diplomas, more specialized training?

The drudgery of daily living and the failures we experience, both by us and toward us, have this in common: they require a vision beyond ourselves if we are to transcend them. In an age of Christian media saturation and an embarrassing wealth of religious resources, it is not more information we need.

It is power.

As has been true of humans in every age, we have need of great, enduring, supernatural, and alien power. What we need cannot come from ourselves, and that is where most religious inspiration fails. And it is why books like *Gospel Formed* by my friend Jeff Medders are not just helpful but needful. We need this book because of the kind of help it provides.

If we go into God's inerrant, infallible, inspired Word looking only for things to do, we will come away with God's good instructions for the good life but without the power to actually follow them. The power to obey does not lie in the commandments. The power to get through the day does not come from the instructions on how to get through it. The power to glorify God is in the glorious gospel, which says not "Do" but "Done!"

Jeff understands this contrast like few others and aims to help us meditate every day on the "Done"-ness of God's work in Christ. The Reverend Maurice Roberts once wrote, "It is the unhurried meditation on gospel truths and the exposing of our minds to these truths that yields the fruit of sanctified character."[1] If this is so—and I believe it is—then Christians today need more and more resources that help us do this, that take us right to the water of the living well and bid us drink deeply. We need more and more resources that show us the gospel in its multitudinous glory. This is what we need, now and ever!

This is why I am grateful for the growing gospel-centered body of literary work in evangelicalism, and why I am grateful for Jeff Medders's contribution to it. In his preaching and pastoral ministry, and from the public platform this ministry has afforded him, Jeff has proven he understands not just the truth of the gospel but the *power* of the gospel as well. He knows that the finished work of Christ is a deep well, beautiful and satisfying and eternally sufficient. Page by page and day by day, his book will give you nothing to drink here but the gospel's living water. In these pages, if you have the eyes to see them, are revealed the things into which even angels long to look (1 Peter 1:12).

Jared C. Wilson

Pastor, Middletown Springs Community Church

Middletown Springs, Vermont

Author, *Gospel Wakefulness* and *Gospel Deeps*

---

1. Maurice Roberts, "O the Depth!" *The Banner of Truth*, July 1990, 2. Quoted in Donald S. Whitney, *Spiritual Disciplines for the Christian Life* (Colorado Springs: Navpress, 1991), 51.

ACKNOWLEDGMENTS

Someone pinch me. I can't believe I'm an author. While my name stands alone as the author, lots of people were a part of making this happen. A big thanks to Chad Rippy and Lawson Flowers. A massive "Thank you!" to Russell Moore, Douglas Wilson, Owen Strachan, and Jimmy Needham for their endorsements. To all of the contributors in the introduction: Thank you! And I couldn't have written this book without the help, support, correction, and encouragement of the following people:

Gary Foster, my agent, and the team at Kregel. Thanks for taking a risk with a first-time, one-bit, scraggly writer.

Jared Wilson. I think your willingness to write the foreword is what made this book shelf-worthy. Your gospel wakefulness is viral. I hope it spreads to the readers (like it did to me).

Brandon Smith. Our friendship is one of Googled Providence. I'm thankful for the many opportunities you've given me to write. You've been so encouraging—too encouraging! You are way gracious with your editing chops. "A gracious editor, who can find?" You, buddy. You.

Natalie. You are my rare jewel. Your love, support, and encouragement keep me going in all of life. Writing, schmiting—the Lord has used you to make me a better man, a more faithful follower of Jesus, and an obsessor of grace. Love you, babe.

Jesus. You are my King, my great God and Savior. You, literally, are my way, truth, and life. I'm so overwhelmed by your grace. Your love for a complete idiot like me is astounding. You are incredible. I love you and your church. I hope this book glorifies you and encourages the saints at large. *Soli Deo Gloria.*

HOW TO USE THIS BOOK

The best way to enjoy *Gospel Formed* is to read one chapter a day. Read more than one if you like—that's cool; don't mind me. Each chapter stands alone but is part of the journey; you are holding expository mutterings that will take you through your worship, community, mission, and identity in Jesus. They shouldn't take long to read—I wrote them to be quick bursts of gospel truth. The introduction, "Gospel Primer," is the longest and by far the most important chapter.

As you read *Gospel Formed*, please do the following for me (and for yourself):

- Read the Bible verse at the top of the page. Don't skip or skim it. It frames what was written and is more helpful than anything I wrote. The goal is to understand, love, and honor God by his Word more and more.
- Read the Bible verses in the notes. There are a lot of them. God's Word is mega-important; take your time and stew in it.
- Read the Bible verse at the end of the chapter. Get the picture? I hope you'll grow in God's Word.
- Pray at the end of each reading. This book is about growing in Christlikeness and drawing near to God, not merely enjoying a parade of gospel-centered jargon. So whatever you do, draw near to God.

Above all, worship Jesus. Make much of Jesus. It's all about him.

Gospel Primer

*Now to him who is able to strengthen you according
to my gospel and the preaching of Jesus Christ . . .*

ROMANS 16:25

The secret to Christian growth is no secret. It's Christ. The cat is out
of the bag. This book is an attempt to follow that cat—the Lion of
Judah.

Every Christian wants to grow and mature in his or her faith,
but sometimes we can't get any traction. We spin our wheels, give
up, and fall back into the proverbial La-Z-Boy of the Christian life.
I've been there, and since you are reading this, I'll bet you have too.
Surely there is more. Right? Of course there is, and it's simple and
jaw-dropping. It sounds too good to be true.

The good news for Christian growth is the Good News. The very
truth that saved you is the same truth that sanctifies you, grows you,
forms you. You grow not by a new method or revelation but by the
old, old story. You don't need new tricks and tactics but the truth of
Jesus, his person, and his work—the gospel.

We grow by the gospel. We grow in the gospel. We grow with
the gospel.[1] Gospel-centeredness is where we need to live. We need
a constant reformation under the gospel of grace.

Jesus died in the place of sinners to grant forgiveness, cleansing,

---

1. "Of this you have heard before in the word of the truth, the gospel, which
has come to you, as indeed in the whole world it is bearing fruit and increasing—
as it also does among you, since the day you heard it and understood the grace
of God in truth" (Col. 1:5–6).

renewal, justification, hope, freedom, and the power to change through his promised Holy Spirit.[2] We don't move on from Jesus. We don't graduate from the gospel. Moving toward gospel-centered living means we never move on from the gospel; rather, its force moves further into our heart. In the long run, devotionals, accountability groups, books, and sermons won't change us—if the gospel is missing. It is the very message of the gospel and the power of the Holy Spirit that changes us.

We need the prescription-strength "preaching of Jesus Christ." In Romans 16:25, the apostle Paul is clear: it's the gospel that makes us strong. Saints require the continual reminder, encouragement, and proclamation of the person and work of Jesus for sinners.

So, Christian—slow down. For real. I hope this entire book helps you to quit laboring in the self-serving salt mines of sanctification and to leap in love for your Lord because of his great love for you. George Müller (1805–1898), faithful pastor, prolific man of prayer, and founder of orphanages in England, recounting his conversion, helps us when he says,

> Apprehending in some measure the love of Jesus for my soul, I was constrained to love Him in return. What all the exhortations and precepts of my father and others could not effect; what all my own resolutions

---

2. *Forgiveness*: "This is my blood of the covenant, which is poured out for many for the forgiveness of sins" (Matt. 26:28). *Cleansing*: "Let us draw near with a true heart in full assurance of faith, with our hearts sprinkled clean from an evil conscience and our bodies washed with pure water" (Heb. 10:22). *Renewal*: "[God] saved us, not because of works done by us in righteousness, but according to his own mercy, by the washing of regeneration and renewal of the Holy Spirit" (Titus 3:5). *Justification*: "[Jesus] was delivered up for our trespasses and raised for our justification" (Rom. 4:25). *Hope*: "Paul, an apostle of Christ Jesus by command of God our Savior and of Christ Jesus our hope . . ." (1 Tim. 1:1). *Freedom*: "For freedom Christ has set us free; stand firm therefore, and do not submit again to a yoke of slavery" (Gal. 5:1). *Power to change*: "But I say, walk by the Spirit, and you will not gratify the desires of the flesh" (Gal. 5:16).

could not bring about, even to renounce a life of sin
and profligacy: I was enabled to do, constrained by
the love of Jesus. The individual who desires to have
his sin forgiven, must seek it through the blood of
Jesus. The individual who desires to get power over
sin, must likewise seek it through the blood of Jesus.[3]

The love of Jesus constrains us, drives us, moves us, changes us,
forms and reforms us. I believe with all my heart that when you start
leaping because of his love, you'll be leaving sin behind and clinging
to your Savior. *That's* Christian growth. My prayer for you is that
you will, as my friend Jared Wilson says, go from "Woe is me!" to
"Whoa is God!"

The Gospel

Before we go on, take some time, right now, and *re*-remember
the gospel. Now is the time to worship.

Jesus. He isn't Diet God, JV God, or God Jr. He is very God of
very God, eternal, all-powerful, Creator and Sustainer.[4] A man from
heaven, who is also God from Galilee, died in your place, for your
sins, he rose from the dead, and Jesus is very much alive today. He
gave you a new life. He justified you. He redeemed you. He cleansed
you. He filled you with the Spirit. He adopted you. He loves you.
He empowers you. He makes you more than a conqueror. He will
never leave you, lose you, or quit loving you.[5]

Is your soul stirring yet?

Let this truth weigh in: You are fully accepted before God, not
because of anything you do or don't do but because of everything

---

3. Roger Steer, *George Müller: Delighted in God* (Fearn, Great Britain: Christian Focus Publications, 2012), 18.

4. "In the beginning was the Word, and the Word was with God, and the Word was God. He was in the beginning with God" (John 1:1–2).

5. Dive into Romans 8 to find all of these great truths.

Jesus did and *is doing* for you right now. God loves you when you are growing in leaps and bounds, and he loves you when you've blown it. Gospel-centered Christians base their hope and joy on the stellar performance of Christ, not their own—or their lack thereof.

To move toward gospel-centeredness means you need to relentlessly rehearse the truths, or *glories*, of the gospel. Remind yourself that apart from Jesus, you can't do a single thing.[6] Soak your heart and mind in the truth that "Christ lives in me" (Gal. 2:20 NLT).

The apostle Paul was convinced that the gospel, the preaching of Jesus, is exactly what you need. Everything else is a placebo. Accept no competitors. Knockoffs will not do. You need the tried-and-true message of God's glory shining at Calvary.

What Is Gospel-Centeredness?

If gospel-centeredness is where we are headed, then what in the world is it? So you don't only take my word for it, I emailed a few top scholars, writers, thinkers, and pastors and asked what they think gospel-centeredness is. Here's what they offered.

Jerry Bridges, author of many gospel-saturated books:

> Being gospel-centered means relying on the shed blood and righteous life of Jesus for our standing and acceptance with God. It means that we seek to obey and serve God out of gratitude for what he has done rather than obeying and serving in an effort to earn his acceptance.

Matt Chandler, pastor, author, and president of Acts 29 Network:

> Being gospel-centered is being empowered by the Holy Spirit not only to understand the robust nature

---

6. "I am the vine; you are the branches. Whoever abides in me and I in him, he it is that bears much fruit, for apart from me you can do nothing" (John 15:5).

of the gospel but also to walk in the implications of
it in every area of our lives—to repeatedly be shaped
and defined by our identity in Christ, and to build
rhythms and structures at home and church that support marveling, cherishing, and being formed by the
gospel message.

Dr. Jim Hamilton of Southern Seminary and author of the pyro-
technically brilliant biblical theology *God's Glory in Salvation
Through Judgment*:

> To be gospel-centered is to believe in the one who,
> though he was rich, became poor for our sake, so that
> by his poverty we might be rich.[7] Gospel-centeredness
> is believing in him and then following him in the
> impoverishing of ourselves for the enrichment of oth-
> ers in Christ.

Sam Storms, pastor and author:

> To be gospel-centered begins with the reality that the
> gospel is not simply the entry point into the Christian
> life but also the foundation and force that shapes all
> we do as followers of Jesus, both in our daily lives and
> in our experience as the corporate body of Christ.
>
> The gospel is the good news of what God has
> graciously done in the incarnation, life, death, and
> resurrection of Jesus Christ to satisfy his own wrath
> and secure the forgiveness of sins and perfect righ-
> teousness for all who trust in Jesus by faith alone.
> The gospel informs, controls, and energizes all we do,
> from the dynamics of interpersonal relationships and

---

7. "For you know the grace of our Lord Jesus Christ, that though he was
rich, yet for your sake he became poor, so that you by his poverty might become
rich" (2 Cor. 8:9).

marriage to work, our use of money, speech, parenting, mission, and all aspects of ministry in the local
church and beyond.

Tim Challies, überblogger and pastor:
To be gospel-centered is to live your life with the constant awareness that the gospel changes everything.
It is to ask in every situation, What difference does
the death and resurrection of Jesus Christ make here
and now?

Douglas Wilson, pastor and prolific author:
I believe in a gospel-centeredness that extends out
to the circumference of all things. The gospel is not
simply a password for getting into heaven. The gospel
is a true explanation of the world.

Dr. Russell Moore, brilliant author and president of the Ethics and
Religious Liberty Commission of the Southern Baptist Convention:
Gospel-centrality means that any aspect of life is
viewed in its cosmic context, in which God is "sum-
ming up" all things in Christ (Eph. 1:10–11). All of
creation is seen in that full context, and connections
are made between everything that is and the kingdom
purposes for which it was called into being. Every
passage of Scripture is interpreted in light of the story
of Jesus, as is every passage of a believer's unfolding
life story.

Owen Strachan, author, professor, and president of the Council of
Biblical Manhood and Womanhood:
The gospel-centered life is one that is driven by the
knowledge that God has redeemed me, a sinner,

through the vicarious death and victorious resurrection of Jesus Christ. The Spirit brings this truth to mind daily, and this daily meditation transforms my life, allowing me to experience power over sin in every area such that I give maximal glory to God as his re-created image-bearer.

Tullian Tchividjian, pastor and author of many grace-laden books: The gospel is God's good-news announcement that Jesus has done for sinners what sinners could never do for themselves. The gospel doxologically declares that because of Christ's finished work for you, you already have all the justification, approval, security, love, worth, meaning, and rescue you long for and look for in a thousand different people and places smaller than Jesus.

The gospel broadcasts the liberating truth that God relates to us based on Jesus' work for us, not our work for him; Jesus' performance for us, not our performance for him. Because Jesus came to secure for us what we could never secure for ourselves, life doesn't have to be a tireless effort to justify ourselves. He came to rescue us from the slavish need to be right, rewarded, regarded, and respected. He came to relieve us of the burden we inherently feel to "get it done." The gospel announces that it's not on me to ensure that the ultimate verdict on my life is pass and not fail.

I hope you are getting the picture. The risen Christ shapes our lives. Gospel-formed people are Jesus-centered people. Here is my attempt to wrestle down a definition using what I like to call a gospel-formed grid.

A Gospel-Formed Grid

Gospel-centeredness means that the person and work of Jesus is the central *message* in all things; he is our *model* for all of life and ministry; the Son of God is our *motivation* in obedience to God's Word; and Jesus of Nazareth is the *means* to carry out all that God commands.

The gospel is a word with many words. It's a message, a proclamation of truth. Jesus is not a side message to the Christian: he is *the* Message, *the* Truth, and *the* Life. It's all about Jesus.

The gospel of Jesus Christ is where we find out who we are as people in Christ Jesus. We start with the gospel message because the gospel of the kingdom informs us how we, as citizens, are to live. We learn our identity from earth-shattering, veil-tearing truths from that place called the Skull—ground zero of the gospel.[8]

While our identity matters, it only matters if we know Jesus' identity—because we are *in Christ*. If we don't think rightly about Jesus, we won't think rightly about ourselves. Jesus is our friend and our Lord. He is the cosmic King, and he's closer than our skin. We ought to fear him, but we should never be afraid of him. The gospel is meant to humble us. And part of the gospel is the glory due Jesus. The glory of Christ needs to take hearts and minds hostage. Jesus is to be exalted over all things in our lives. We are not the ones who have been given a name at which every knee will bow (Phil. 2:9–11).

The person and work of Jesus fuels gospel-formed lives. No one can hear too often that Jesus is our great God and Savior, he has made us his people, and he is purifying us for his glory and our good (Titus 2:13–14). Jesus is the rocket fuel of the Christian experience, of life "in Christ." And he's the destination. We will be with him forever, and we are being formed into his image. I'm convinced, more and more, that we need the teaching of Jesus Christ brought to

---

8. "And he went out, bearing his own cross, to the place called The Place of a Skull, which in Aramaic is called Golgotha. There they crucified him, and with him two others, one on either side, and Jesus between them" (John 19:17–18).

our weak and trembling hearts. Paul, at the end of Romans, writes, "Now to him who is able to *strengthen* you according to my gospel and the preaching of Jesus Christ . . ." (Rom. 16:25, italics mine). God himself makes us strong. He does the strengthening. But what does God use? He uses the message of Jesus, the gospel of grace, to transform us. And this is available to Christians everywhere. No seminary credentials needed. No spiritual pedigree required. Christ is available to us all. And he is who we need.

I once was privy to a conversation I'll never forget. Over a tasty lunch, a fellow clergyman confessed his pain and heartache to pastor, scholar, and author Ray Ortlund. I was on the edge of my seat to hear Ray's response. His steady, hope-filled eyes looked into the other man's eyes, and softly and firmly he said, "Brother, Jesus loves you."

Powerful. We need more of that. *I need more of that.*

While *message* focuses on right thinking, *motivation* hones in on right doing for the right reasons. Jesus shapes what we do and *why* we do it. The gospel compels us to seek and grant forgiveness with one another *as God in Christ* forgave us (Eph. 4:32). The gospel reveals to us that we are no longer our own; we belong to Jesus. Now we make it our aim to honor and please him (1 Cor. 6:20; 2 Cor. 5:9). The glories of Calvary ignite in Christians a mad dash away from sin, but not simply to avoid getting in trouble—also to enjoy God and glorify Jesus forever.

I've heard Christians say (and I know I've said it before too), "I'm waiting to be freed/released/saved from _____." Is that truly biblical? I think the satanic forces conjured up that formula and have been peddling it in accountability groups since the nineties Christians are not waiting to be freed from sin. Here's why: a man from Galilee once screamed, "It is finished!"

Our brother Paul writes:

> We know that our old self was crucified with him
> in order that the body of sin might be brought to

nothing, so that we would no longer be enslaved to sin. For one who has died has been set free from sin. Now if we have died with Christ, we believe that we will also live with him. We know that Christ, being raised from the dead, will never die again; death no longer has dominion over him. For the death he died he died to sin, once for all, but the life he lives he lives to God. So you also must consider yourselves dead to sin and alive to God in Christ Jesus.

Let not sin therefore reign in your mortal body, to make you obey its passions. Do not present your members to sin as instruments for unrighteousness, but present yourselves to God as those who have been brought from death to life, and your members to God as instruments for righteousness. For sin will have no dominion over you, since you are not under law but under grace. (Rom. 6:6–14)

So why should we flee sin? We've been brought from death to life. Why won't sin bully us any longer? We're under grace. The chains don't need re-breaking. We need renewed minds (Rom. 12:1–2) and re-fixated eyes on our encouraging Christ (Heb. 12:1–2). The gospel motivates us to pursue holiness because we are free, and where the Spirit of the Lord is there is freedom (2 Cor. 3:17).

Jesus isn't only about what we shouldn't do; he is also about us moving into the things we should do. The gospel motivates us to flee sin—yes and amen!—and the work of Jesus invites us toward the good works that Jesus has prepared for us to walk in (Eph. 2:10). What was Jesus' motivation in his life and ministry? "Hallowed be your name." What is ours? "Hallowed be your name." The Holy Spirit gifts us for good works so that "God may be glorified through Jesus Christ" (1 Peter 4:10–11).

If the gospel is our message and our motivation for obedience, it is also our *model*. Here we see that Jesus models for us the right attitudes, tones, and heart-posture in all of life. The gospel gives the reason (motivation) and the rhythm (model).

How should a husband and wife relate? In accordance with the model God provides in the gospel: Jesus and his church (Eph. 5:22–33). All Christian virtue is modeled and made known to us by the Jesus of Matthew, Mark, Luke, and John. If we want to be more loving, humble, and selfless—there is nowhere better to look than the foot-washing, ever-patient, always-compassionate, ultra-caring Jesus Christ who loved us sinners at the cross (John 15:13).

Up to this point, everything sounds all fine and dandy, but a question looms: "How am I *really* going to change? How can I do all this? I fail often. I struggle. I want to change and grow, but my goodness—this seems beyond me. I want a gospel-formed life. I want my life to be all about Jesus, but I don't even know where to start."

Brothers and sisters, let me encourage you: You are right—you cannot do this. None of us can. This kind of life is way beyond our horsepower. But the good news is that it isn't beyond Jesus. It *is* Jesus. We cannot forget our gospel *means*: the One who now lives in us (Gal. 2:20). The means, muscle, capacity, and know-how of the Christian life lie not in our personal sufficiency but in Jesus. And if we are in Christ and Christ is in us, then the power for the Christian life is now *in* us. The Holy Spirit of God is rumbling through our lives—and he will bear fruit, he will help us cry out, "Abba!" We unspectacular Christians work in concert with the glorious Spirit of the Christ (Phil. 2:12–13). We are totally at the mercy of our merciful Lord. Is there a better place to be?

A gospel-formed life has Jesus as our message, our motivation, our model, and our means. All of this matters because the worship of Jesus is the goal of the gospel.

Worship Is the Aim

My goal for *Gospel Formed* is to serve you in the worship of God. Some of the chapters will be punchy, and some of what you read will be irritating, because truth is known for going against the grain. If you grew up in the Bible Belt (like me), there are lots of grains that need some going against. Grace does that.

The ultimate aim of this little book is to crank your worship of Jesus up to eleven. Only God can do this in you, and only the glories of his gospel are able to ignite our hearts to worship in spirit and in truth, not just words. Our Christian culture's gospel-centered jive is in danger of being a dance with no soul or a Quick-E-Mart chemical cake passed off as Aunt Betty's homemade Chocolate Cardiac Hero: a complete fake. Being gospel-centered in language and theology isn't enough. Pharisees can yack away with hyphen-ated gospel-talk, but we are after the *spirit and truth* of gospel-centeredness: worship.

My deep prayer over this project is that these expository mut-terings would stir our hearts to rejoice over our great God and King, our Lion and Lamb, our Savior and Friend. Let's worship Jesus. There is a reason why we ought to beat the gospel-centered drum again and again, and then some more. The Bible gives us ample motivation to worship Jesus. It's called the gospel.

We Worship Jesus Because . . .

We worship Jesus because "he is the radiance of the glory of God and the exact imprint of his nature, and he upholds the universe by the word of his power" (Heb. 1:3).

We harp on the gospel because "for our sake he made him to be sin who knew no sin, so that in him we might become the righteousness of God" (2 Cor. 5:21).

Our hope is wrapped up in the truth that "he was pierced for our transgressions; he was crushed for our iniquities; upon him was the chastisement that brought us peace, and with his wounds we are healed" (Isa. 53:5).

We center our lives on Jesus because "we know that Christ, being raised from the dead, will never die again; death no longer has dominion over him" (Rom. 6:9).

We sing, sacrifice, and follow Jesus because "there is one God, and there is one mediator between God and men, the man Christ Jesus" (1 Tim. 2:5).

We go on gospel mission because "the saying is trustworthy and deserving of full acceptance, that Christ Jesus came into the world to save sinners" (1 Tim. 1:15).

We have confidence in life and death because of Jesus, "who gave himself for our sins to deliver us from the present evil age, according to the will of our God and Father, to whom be the glory forever and ever. Amen" (Gal. 1:4–5).

We walk with joy and no condemnation because "he himself bore our sins in his body on the tree, that we might die to sin and live to righteousness. By his wounds you have been healed" (1 Peter 2:24).

We know we are saved because "he entered once for all into the holy places, not by means of the blood of goats and calves but by means of his own blood, thus securing an eternal redemption" (Heb. 9:12).

Jesus is our great reward and love because "in him we have redemption through his blood, the forgiveness of our trespasses, according to the riches of his grace" (Eph. 1:7).

And lastly, *we are gospel-centered because* "though he was in the form of God, did not count equality with God a thing to be grasped, but emptied himself, by taking the form of a servant, being born in the likeness of men. And being found in human form, he humbled himself by becoming obedient to the point of death, even death on a cross. Therefore God has highly exalted him and bestowed on him the name that is above every name, so that at the name of Jesus every knee should bow, in heaven and on earth and under the earth, and every tongue confess that Jesus Christ is Lord, to the glory of God the Father" (Phil. 2:6–11).

That's why we worship Jesus! It's all about Jesus.

Here is my prayer for you (and I hope you'll pray it too): that over the course of these pages, you'll be drawn deeper into the treasure trove of the gospel and be immersed in the greatness of Christ—his awesomeness and his love. We can't comprehend the magnitude of grace unless God guides us into it (Eph. 3:16–19). The Puritan theologian Thomas Manton was right in saying, "The gospel is God's riddle, which none but himself can expound. Beg the Spirit of revelation; you cannot have a knowledge of it without a revelation from Christ."[9] We need the Spirit of Jesus in order to behold Jesus. He can do that work in us. Today, even. Is this too much to ask of our lavish God? No way. Let's pray that he will do more than we could even ask, think, or imagine.[10]

Throughout the rest of this book, I hope we can look at the gospel and our lives, where the bloody cross meets the road we travel. Since the gospel is our message, model, motivation, and means, the gospel informs and shapes our worship, identity, community, and mission. In two foundational New Testament passages—the Great Commission in Matthew 28, and Acts chapter 1—we see examples of how the crucified and risen Jesus brings this about (italics mine in the following):

> Now the eleven disciples went to Galilee, to the mountain to which Jesus had directed them. And when they saw him they *worshiped him*, but some doubted. And Jesus came and said to them, "All authority in heaven and on earth has been given to me. Go therefore

---

9. Thomas Manton, *The Complete Works of Thomas Manton*, vol. 11 (London: James Nisbet & Co., 1873), 134.

10. "Now to him who is able to do far more abundantly than all that we ask or think, according to the power at work within us . . ." (Eph. 3:20).

and *make disciples* of all nations, baptizing them in the name of the Father and of the Son and of the Holy Spirit, *teaching them to observe all that I have commanded you.* And behold, I am with you always, to the end of the age." (Matt. 28:16–20)

You will receive power when the Holy Spirit has come upon you, and *you will be my witnesses* in Jerusalem and in all Judea and Samaria, and to the end of the earth. (Acts 1:8)

The disciples *worship* the risen Jesus. Jesus establishes them as a *community*—the eleven disciples are together in following Jesus and in teaching others how to follow Jesus because Jesus said, "If you love me, you will keep my commandments" (John 14:15). The Lord then gives them a new *identity*: witnesses. And their *mission* is to take the name of Jesus worldwide. Worship, identity, community, and mission are all rooted in the gospel of the kingdom.

As you dive into this book, I hope to be a mere tour guide. We'll look at a text and I'll make some comments, hopefully directing your gaze to our crucified King, and if I do my job, you'll forget I'm even here. We'll look at gospel worship, our gospel identity, the meaning of gospel community, and our charge for the gospel mission.

Now let's plumb the depths of the wall-to-wall glories of the gospel together. And let's always, only, and totally worship our King of kings.

Like newborn infants, long for the pure spiritual milk, that by it you may grow up into salvation— if indeed you have tasted that the Lord is good.

1 PETER 2:2–3

PART ONE

The Gospel Starting Block

The gospel, Jesus' death and resurrection for our sins, is our starting block and our anchor and our wings.

The gospel is our center, our core, our fuel. It's our framework for understanding reality

CHAPTER 1

The Main Thing

I decided to know nothing among you except
Jesus Christ and him crucified.

1 CORINTHIANS 2:2

Have you ever heard of a pew rat? It's a kid-like creature that grew up on SunnyD and the Goldfish cracker crumbs found in the church carpet.

For as long as I can remember, I've been around a church. If our local church's doors were open, my family was there. I knew the blueprints of the church like I knew the maze on the back of my cereal box. Every Sunday morning, Sunday night, and Wednesday night, in a large room with an illuminated cross looming behind the preacher, I sat there, week after week. I was a pew rat.

Yet even with exponential hours of exposure to the Bible, a cross, a baptistery, and ice-cream socials in the fellowship hall—even after countless sermons and Sunday school lessons—I totally missed what Christianity is all about.

Is that you too? Or maybe you've never set foot in a church, or you are new to this Christianity thing, or you've been a Christian for some time but you've gotten sick of all the glitz, glam, frills, and hoopla. I'm with you. And I hope you won't be too shocked by what you are about to read. Though maybe you should be. I was when I first read it. I still feel the jolt.

One truth in the Bible is more important than the rest. I love the Bible and all its truths. And I believe every single word is inspired by

God and important, even the ones in the second half of the book of Numbers. But there is *one* truth of utmost importance. The others aren't trivial—by no means!—but this one truth is a big one, and I believe it with all my heart. Why? Because the apostle Paul said so. If he told me to jump off a bridge, I'd do it.

In everything Paul wrote—more than half of the New Testament letters are his—he says the good *news* is the front-page headline. "For I delivered to you as of *first importance* what I also received: that Christ died for our sins in accordance with the Scriptures, that he was buried, that he was raised on the third day in accordance with the Scriptures" (1 Cor. 15:3–4, italics mine).

> The gospel is the center of the Bible, and it ought to be the center of our lives, homes, churches, ministries, spiritual disciplines, songs, parenting, marriages, jobs — *everything*.

God says the gospel is the most important truth in his word. "First importance" (or "most important," NLT), means that the gospel is the leading truth of the Bible; it's at the head of the pack, the alpha truth, and all other biblical truths fall in line behind it. The gospel is the mama duck in our gaggle of doctrine. She leads, she guides, and all other doctrine looks to her, follows her, and keeps in step with her. To live a Christian life is to live "in step with the truth of the gospel" (Gal. 2:14) and to "let your manner of life be worthy of the gospel of Christ" (Phil. 1:27). The Christian life is formed by the glories of the gospel—it's patterned and powered by the gospel of grace in all of life, for the rest of life.

The gospel is the center of the Bible, and it ought to be the center of our lives, homes, churches, ministries, spiritual disciplines, songs, parenting, marriages, jobs—*everything*.

The focal point of the Christian life is one cross and one empty tomb. Without the gospel, we lack the proper understanding of any doctrine, and especially a robust knowing of God himself. "The gospel," Michael Bird, author and systematic theologian, says, "is the nexus into the reality of the God who has revealed himself."[1] If we want to know the glory of God, his high-definition glory is found in the gospel of Jesus—for Jesus makes God known (John 1:18). The cross is our logo. It's the power of our lives, because Christ is alive in us.[2] Husbands and wives pattern their marriage after the gospel (Eph. 5:22–33). Christian interaction is gospel driven.[3] Humility is possible for us proud people because of Jesus at work in us (Phil. 2:1–11).[4] The gospel is the message of the church.[5] Christians are made strong because of the gospel.[6] Bird is right: "We need a gospel-driven theology in order to yield a gospel-soaked piety and a gospel-acting church."[7]

It's all gospel. All the time. A gospel party don't stop.

The gospel, the news of the eternal Son of God dying in our place for our sins, is not only the center of the Bible; it's also the center of history. In God's gospel, he is reconciling all things unto himself for the praise of his glory.[8] Nothing compares to the glory

---

1. Michael F. Bird, *Evangelical Theology: A Biblical and Systematic Introduction* (Grand Rapids: Zondervan, 2013), 41.

2. "I have been crucified with Christ. It is no longer I who live, but Christ who lives in me. And the life I now live in the flesh I live by faith in the Son of God, who loved me and gave himself for me" (Gal. 2:20).

3. "Be kind to one another, tenderhearted, forgiving one another, as God in Christ forgave you" (Eph. 4:32).

4. "Have this mind among yourselves, which is yours in Christ Jesus" (Phil. 2:5).

5. "Him we proclaim, warning everyone and teaching everyone with all wisdom, that we may present everyone mature in Christ" (Col. 1:28).

6. "Now to him who is able to strengthen you according to my gospel and the preaching of Jesus Christ, according to the revelation of the mystery that was kept secret for long ages" (Rom. 16:25).

7. Bird, *Evangelical Theology*, 41.

8. "In him we have redemption through his blood, the forgiveness of our trespasses, according to the riches of his grace, which he lavished upon us, in all

of the gospel in giving glory to God—and God will never get tired of the gospel; it's the soundtrack of the heavenly places (Rev. 5:1–14). The angels, who have seen things we can't even fathom, looked at the bloody cross and the empty tomb with sheer excitement. Peter tells us,

> Concerning this salvation, the prophets who prophesied about the grace that was to be yours searched and inquired carefully, inquiring what person or time the Spirit of Christ in them was indicating when he predicted the sufferings of Christ and the subsequent glories. It was revealed to them that they were serving not themselves but you, in the things that have now been announced to you through those who preached the good news to you by the Holy Spirit sent from heaven, things into which angels long to look. (1 Peter 1:10–12)

Do you long to look into the gospel? When you hear the gospel preached, do you perk up? I can relate to being bored by a lecture on some theological abstraction from a land far, far away, but not by the gospel; the wildness of the gospel vaporizes yawning and boredom. There is a shock-and-awe that comes with the gospel. God loves the gospel. The angels are giddy over it. If you don't quite get the fireworks of the gospel, preach the gospel to yourself. Like Paul prayed for the Ephesians, pray

> that the God of our Lord Jesus Christ, the Father of glory, may give you the Spirit of wisdom and of

---

wisdom and insight making known to us the mystery of his will, according to his purpose, which he set forth in Christ as a plan for the fullness of time, to unite all things in him, things in heaven and things on earth" (Eph. 1:7–10).

revelation in the knowledge of him, having the eyes
of your hearts enlightened, that you may know what
is the hope to which he has called you, what are the
riches of his glorious inheritance in the saints, and
what is the immeasurable greatness of his power
toward us who believe, according to the working of
his great might that he worked in Christ when he
raised him from the dead and seated him at his right
hand in the heavenly places. (Eph. 1:17–20)

Pray that the main thing will be *your* main thing. Pray to be
gospel-centered, because you know how easy it is to get off-kilter.
There's more than one way to skin a faith.
It doesn't take long to forget the gospel.
As D.A. Carson noted, "one generation
believes the gospel, the next assumes it,
and the following generation denies it."[9]
We must strive to make the good news
the core message we put forth, the chief
model we emulate, the leading moti-

> **There's more than one way to skin a faith. It doesn't take long to forget the gospel.**

vation in obedience, and the proprietary means of growth in the
Christian life. Anything else falls dreadfully, woefully short.

"Keep the main thing, the main thing." I've heard a gazillion
people say that—and they're right.[10] We must labor to keep the
main thing, the main thing. Let the main thing be the subject of
your life, not various theologies, sanctifi-cannots,[11] translation wars,
musical styles, or whatever else you want to obsess over. Those are
fine discussions, but they make a poor center.

9. D.A. Carson, *Basics for Believers: An Exposition of Philippians* (Grand Rapids: Baker, 1996), 26–27.
10. It's possible Stephen Covey (*First Things First*, 1994) said it first.
11. Sanctification is more than hammering on what we cannot and should not do—it's also doing good works, encouraging others, etc.

Yet while the gospel is the main thing, don't forget about those other things. One of the dangers of being gospel-centered is neglecting what surrounds the center. You can't have a true center without surroundings. Gospel-centered ministries, books, and blogs are great at not missing the forest for the trees, the metanarrative of God's redemptive grace from cover to cover, but don't forget the trees for the forest. We need to be both forest and bark enthusiasts. The Bible is a holistic ecosystem; all of its verses live one off of another. That's why gospel-saturated Christians will read the book of Leviticus—because it's a part of what God has given us, which can make us wise to his saving work.[12] Gospel-centrality is an attempt to make the gospel the focal point, not to neglect everything else in the circle.

In 1 Corinthians 2:2, Paul wanted to make the gospel known among the Corinthians—and nothing else: "For I decided to know nothing among you except Jesus Christ and him crucified." But if you are familiar with the Corinthian letters, then you know that Paul taught more subjects—way more—than the gospel alone. How does this align with gospel-centeredness? Paul taught not in *exclusion* to the gospel but in *relation* to the gospel; not in *addition* to the gospel but as an *explanation* from the gospel. All Christian teaching should be an exposition of the gospel. Everything Paul teaches about marriage, spiritual gifts, the Trinity, communion, church discipline, love, idolatry, and holiness either springs from the truth of the gospel or comes back around to it. Everything connects to the gospel. But while the glorious news of Jesus is of first importance, it is not of only importance.

If we don't talk about the pursuit of holiness—and actually

---

12. "From childhood you have been acquainted with the sacred writings, which are able to make you wise for salvation through faith in Christ Jesus" (2 Tim. 3:15).

pursue it—then we aren't centered on the gospel.[13] We can't be gospel-centered and ignore inerrancy, eternal torment in hell, the complementary nature of manhood and womanhood, biblical church membership, and church discipline. Gospel-centrality is a holistic approach to the Christian life, and it doesn't breed apathy toward the rest of the Bible; if anything, it ignites a passion for all that the Bible says, because it's all about Jesus.[14]

It's not anti-gospel-centered to discuss the end times, but it is if you *never* do. It's in the Bible. Mull over it. Paul even says that end-times doctrine is meant to encourage your heart,[15] not

> **View everything in relation to the gospel; teach and be taught the *whole* counsel of God.**

elevate its beats per minute. View everything in relation to the gospel; teach and be taught the *whole* counsel of God. Don't dismiss other important truths—just keep the gospel as the blazing center of your theological solar system. If you are going to occupy anything, sit in the glories of the gospel—the death of Jesus in the place of sinners, and his rising again to give new life to all who believe. Jesus came to save sinners—glory to God![16] Which is the point of the

13. "For the grace of God has appeared, bringing salvation for all people, training us to renounce ungodliness and worldly passions, and to live self-controlled, upright, and godly lives in the present age, waiting for our blessed hope, the appearing of the glory of our great God and Savior Jesus Christ, who gave himself for us to redeem us from all lawlessness and to purify for himself a people for his own possession who are zealous for good works" (Titus 2:11–14)

14. "You search the Scriptures because you think that in them you have eternal life; and it is they that bear witness about me" (John 5:39) "Beginning with Moses and all the Prophets, he interpreted to them in all the Scriptures the things concerning himself" (Luke 24:27).

15. "Then we who are alive, who are left, will be caught up together with them in the clouds to meet the Lord in the air, and so we will always be with the Lord. Therefore *encourage* one another with these words" (1 Thess. 4:17–18).

16. "The saying is trustworthy and deserving of full acceptance, that Christ Jesus came into the world to save sinners, of whom I am the foremost" (1 Tim. 1:15).

gospel: God being glorified. The gospel is not the endgame of the gospel; God is.

Jesus' work on the cross gave us life, peace, community, forgiveness—he lavishes his people with good things. And the prime lavishness, the reward of rewards, is God himself. Isn't that why Jesus tore the veil? "For Christ also suffered once for sins, the righteous for the unrighteous, that he might bring us to God" (1 Peter 3:18).

Salvation is only salvation because God is the reward. Eternal life is joyous and good because it is with the Eternal One. Heaven isn't heavenly because of its location; God's glorious enjoyableness is what makes heaven, heaven. His radiating presence is the zoning code for heaven. God makes all things awesome. God is the chief reward of the gospel, and all other gifts are from him. He is omni-benevolent. Every blessing we taste comes from God's kitchen, prepared by his hands, served up for us to enjoy. "Every good gift and every perfect gift is from above, coming down from the Father of lights" (James 1:17). Like a master chef, he brings handcrafted delights for all the little former orphans, now beloved children he calls his own.

Gospel-centered Christians are God-enjoying, God-centered, Jesus-exalting, Spirit-loving, Bible-devouring Christians. We don't worship the gospel; we worship the God of the gospel. The gospel is God's act of turning scoundrels into saints, turning sin-seekers into people who now find their utmost satisfaction in God.

"God is the strength of my heart and my portion forever" (Ps. 73:26). One day our bodies will fail. Our hearts will quit on us. And all of our stuff will be worthless. Everything we once could buy and enjoy, touch, taste, shoot, grill, read, and watch will be shelved, sold, or trashed. After our lungs deflate, there will be only one thing that remains for us—the Three in One.

God is the overriding and underwriting joy of gospel-soaked saints. The gospel gives what moth and rust—and death—cannot destroy. We get God.

Be engrossed by grace. Be engulfed in grace. Nothing deserves our obsession like the gospel. Keep it. Guard it. Enjoy it. Behold your God.

May you, by all means necessary, keep the main thing, the main thing.

Far be it from me to boast except in the cross
of our Lord Jesus Christ, by which the world has
been crucified to me, and I to the world.

GALATIANS 6:14

CHAPTER 2

God Commands Gospel-Centeredness

And you, who once were alienated and hostile in mind, doing evil deeds, he has now reconciled in his body of flesh by his death, in order to present you holy and blameless and above reproach before him, if indeed you continue in the faith, stable and steadfast, not shifting from the hope of the gospel that you heard, which has been proclaimed in all creation under heaven, and of which I, Paul, became a minister.

COLOSSIANS 1:21–23

I'm not fluent in any language other than English. Being half Mexican, and having been born and raised in the great state of Texas, I can stumble through some Spanish. Oh, and I can speak a wee bit of Thai from two mission trips—nothing to write home about. English is the only language I'm proficient at. So what would it be like for me to wake up from a nap and find that I can't speak anything but Swedish—or remember a thing about my life? I can't imagine it.

Yet that is what actually happened to Michael Boatwright.

In February 2013, Boatwright, a Navy veteran from Florida, was found unconscious in a motel in California. He awakened days later in a hospital with no memory of his past, speaking only in Swedish and claiming that his name was Johan Ek. Exercise clothes, tennis rackets, and four forms of ID, all saying Michael Thomas Boatwright, were all he had with him.

It turned out that Michael had lived in Sweden off and on for about twenty years. But he couldn't remember any of it. Doctors thought he suffered from transient global amnesia, which is typically brought on by a traumatic event, though such an incident was another thing Michael couldn't remember. His first look in a mirror brought tears to his eyes: he didn't recognize his own face. Living in the United States made Michael feel like a stranger in his own country because he could no longer speak the language.

So he moved to Sweden, where he hoped to make a full recovery, remember who he was, and rebuild his life. To all appearances, things had turned around for him and were going well. Yet sadly, in April 2014, Michael Boatwright was found dead in his home, a victim of suicide at age sixty-two.[1]

Boatwright's story is shocking. Suddenly he forgot everything about Michael Boatwright and became, in his mind, Johan Ek. It was a seismic shift so shattering that it forced Boatwright to rebuild his life and struggle to reclaim who he once was. He wanted to find his center, his reality, because he had drifted into unreality. He didn't want to be Johan Ek; he wanted to be who he really was.

There's a lesson in Michael Boatwright's strange and tragic story. If we aren't careful, we too can drift from reality—the reality of grace alone, Jesus alone, the cross and empty tomb alone. If we don't keep a close watch on ourselves and our beliefs (1 Tim. 4:16), a bout of theological amnesia can leave us speaking

> **If we aren't careful, we too can drift from reality – the reality of grace alone, Jesus alone, the cross and empty tomb alone.**

---

1. Elizabeth Landau, Per Nyberg, and William Hudson, "Michael Boatwright, Navy Vet with Amnesia, Arrives in Sweden to Rebuild Life," CNN, August 21, 2013, http://www.cnn.com/2013/08/21/health/amnesia-swedish/; Brett Kelman, "Michael Boatwright Found Dead in Sweden," *Desert Sun*, April 23, 2014, http://www.desertsun.com/story/news/2014/04/23/michael-boatwright -dead-amnesia-sweden-palm-springs/8055511/.

moralism and legalism and living like a foreigner to the gospel of the kingdom of Christ. We must resolve to center ourselves on the gospel. We must re-remember its glories that shape our identity and activity.

Is gospel-centeredness a big deal? Yes and no. The term is fresh and it's great, but it's not what matters; the concept is king, and it has been around forever. The Trinity is gospel-centered. God's whole plan of redemption is gospel-centered. Before the foundation of the world, the triune God wrote a book with all the names of those who would be saved by the Lamb, by his blood, by grace through faith.[2] God has been about the gospel for a long time. Gospel-centered Christianity is nonnegotiable; God commands it.

In Colossians 1:23, Paul says we are to "continue in the faith, stable and steadfast, not shifting from the hope of the gospel that you heard." God doesn't want us to swerve away from the hope of the gospel. Churches, ministries, seminaries, parachurch organizations, Sunday school classes, and committed churchgoers can all shift from the center: the hope of the gospel. With all of your might, vigor, resolve, and strength—remain firm in the gospel. Don't shift.

A Christianity filled with well-intended good advice, severed from the good news, is bad news and bad advice. The gospel of the kingdom is concerned with making Jesus' people into holy people (Titus 2:14). But when we want an earthly power to accomplish what only divine power can do, we shift from the gospel. We need the extraterrestrial power of our once-dead Prince of Peace. The

---

2. "The one who conquers will be clothed thus in white garments, and I will never blot his name out of the book of life. I will confess his name before my Father and before his angels" (Rev. 3:5). "[Their names were] written before the foundation of the world in the book of life of the Lamb who was slain" (Rev. 13:8). "The beast that you saw was, and is not, and is about to rise from the bottomless pit and go to destruction. And the dwellers on earth whose names have not been written in the book of life from the foundation of the world will marvel to see the beast, because it was and is not and is to come" (Rev. 17:8).

hope for change isn't found in our own strength but in the strength of Jesus. Going to church doesn't change anything—Jesus does, and he works through his Word and his people.

The hope of the gospel is the solid Rock, Jesus himself. When we are weak, he is strong. When we are confused, he is sober-minded. When we feel absolutely devastated and crushed by our continual ineptness to be Christlike, we hear, "My brothers, you also have died to the law through the body of Christ, so that you may belong to another, to him who has been raised from the dead, in order that we may bear fruit for God" (Rom. 7:4). Don't start thinking that your good works are adding anything to the work of Christ. Don't start believing that somehow God is going to love you more because of what you are doing or not doing. Cement the truth in your heart that you are fully forgiven for all of your crimes against God because of Jesus. Don't forget that you are divorced from sin's power because you are married to Christ.

Far too often, we live and think like the Galatians, who began with the gospel of grace but drifted into works. "Let me ask you only this," Paul wrote to them. "Did you receive the Spirit by works of the law or by hearing with faith? Are you so foolish? Having begun by the Spirit, are you now being perfected by the flesh?" (Gal. 3:2–3).

Remember, you are not beyond shifting from the gospel, nor am I, and it would be ungospel-centered to think of ourselves more highly than we ought.[3] Even Peter and Barnabas shifted for a second. Paul said, "I saw that their conduct was not in step with the truth of the gospel" (Gal. 2:14). Shifting from the center is quite possible, and it doesn't always resemble transient global amnesia. It's more like the slow-mo pull of playing in the ocean: before you

---

3. "By the grace given to me I say to everyone among you not to think of himself more highly than he ought to think, but to think with sober judgment, each according to the measure of faith that God has assigned" (Rom. 12:3).

know it, your towel, flip-flops, orthodoxy, and joy are nowhere in sight.

When you shift from the gospel there are four places you can drift into: license, legalism, lukewarmness, or leaving the faith altogether. You may not have a life of rampant sin, but you may have an area of license that is just as sinister. Legalism will take you into self-righteousness and works-based approval. You'll start to gauge your joy on yourself and not on Christ, and you'll begin to hope in the branch rather than the Vine.

Lukewarm describes a commitment to Jesus at a microscopic level. It's there in word but not deed. Lukewarmness isn't that tricky to diagnose. Jesus says, "Because you are lukewarm, and neither hot nor cold, I will spit you out of my mouth. For you say, I am rich, I have prospered, and I need nothing, not realizing that you are wretched, pitiable, poor, blind, and naked" (Rev. 3:16–17). Being lukewarm isn't just having a low, flickering passion for Jesus. It's thinking, "I'm okay without him." We don't remember our consistent need for Christ. Lukewarmness is a subtle, stealth-state of the heart that says, "Jesus? Who? Oh yeah, Jesus. Of course I need him." It has the resemblance of commitment to Jesus, but it's much like a forged Leonardo da Vinci or a dreamy Hollywood couple on their fourth Vegas wedding—it's hardly serious. Jesus is an afterthought, a tip-of-the-hat. Jesus is grossed out by that style of Christianity (Rev. 3:16).

> God's arms are open. He is the prodigal's father, yours and mine.

The good news is that you can come back. God's arms are open. He is the prodigal's father, yours and mine. Jesus instructs the lukewarm, "I counsel you to buy from me gold refined by fire, so that you may be rich, and white garments so that you may clothe yourself and the shame of your nakedness may not be seen, and salve to anoint your eyes, so that you may see" (Rev. 3:18). The remedy? Revisit the glories of the gospel: the riches of grace, the righteousness of Jesus freely given to us, the covering of our shame, the opening of our eyes. We obtain these priceless treasures at no cost to us—they are given freely to us by his grace (Isa. 55:1–2). Charles Spurgeon, preaching on the Lord's words from Revelation, said, "Gospel riches are sent to remove our wretchedness, and mercy to remove our misery."[4] We get our souls hemmed back in by the riches of grace.

If you've shifted, look back to Jesus. He's still off the cross, he's still out of the tomb, and he's still on the throne. Remember that Christ alone, and none of your works, makes you righteous before God. That ought to crank up your heart, revoke any license, and pluck out the legalism.

May the hope of the gospel be etched into your heart today, tomorrow, and always.

Him we proclaim, warning everyone and teaching everyone with all wisdom, that we may present everyone mature in Christ. For this I toil, struggling with all his energy that he powerfully works within me.

COLOSSIANS 1:28–29

------

4. C.H. Spurgeon, *The Metropolitan Tabernacle Pulpit Sermons*, vol. 29 (London: Passmore & Alabaster, 1883), 341.

PART TWO

What Is
Gospel Worship?

Gospel worship is the glorifying of God in all of life, in light of, in accordance with, motivated by, and empowered by the gospel of grace.

Gospel worship is living in response to the gospel in spirit and in truth.

CHAPTER 3

Gospel Worship

*The men marveled, saying, "What sort of man is
this, that even winds and sea obey him?"*

MATTHEW 8:27

Think of the loudest thunderclap you've ever heard. Are you hearing it again? I heard a clap last year that I could also feel—it rattled my house and my bones.

Imagine that kind of thunder, add some piercing rain and a barrage of lightning, and then place yourself not in the safety of your home but in a rickety boat in the middle of a Galilean sea that's heaving like an upset stomach. Remember this story? "They went and woke him, saying, 'Save us, Lord; we are perishing.' And he said to them, 'Why are you afraid, O you of little faith?' Then he rose and rebuked the winds and the sea, and there was a great calm" (Matt. 8:25 26).

The disciples are having a complete meltdown. And Jesus? He's snoozing. They wake him up, and then this man from Nazareth *rebukes* the storm. Let that sink into your rusty imagination. Jesus *speaks* to a storm—and it hears him. *And* it follows orders—instantly. How would you respond to that? (I can't even get my dog to listen to me.) Here's how the disciples responded: "The men marveled, saying, 'What sort of man is this, that even winds and sea obey him?'" (v. 27).

Answer their question. What sort of man is Jesus of Nazareth? The answer is the foundation for all of life—and for your eternity.

Jesus is 100 percent God. He isn't some diluted, knockoff version of God, nor is he a man who became God. Jesus is fully God and fully man, and we are to worship him as such. C.S. Lewis, responding to a letter, wrote,

> The most striking thing about Our Lord is the union of great ferocity with extreme tenderness. . . . Add to this that He is also a supreme ironist, dialectician, and (occasionally) humourist. So go on! You are on the right track now: getting to the real Man behind all the plaster dolls that have been substituted for Him. This is the appearance in Human form of the God who made the Tiger *and* the Lamb, the avalanche *and* the rose. He'll frighten and puzzle you: but the real Christ *can* be loved and admired as the doll can't.[1]

We need a big *and* accessible view of Jesus—the Lord of the cosmos who will bounce a kid on his knee and raise a friend from the dead. We must behold the Colossal Christ whom Paul describes in Colossians 1. Who is Jesus? This is Jesus:

> He is the image of the invisible God, the firstborn of all creation. For by him all things were created, in heaven and on earth, visible and invisible, whether thrones or dominions or rulers or authorities—all things were created through him and for him. And he is before all things, and in him all things hold together. And he is the head of the body, the church. He is the beginning, the firstborn from the dead, that in everything he might be preeminent. For in

---

1. C.S. Lewis, *The Collected Letters of C.S. Lewis*, vol. 3 (New York: Harper-Collins, 2007), 1,011.

him all the fullness of God was pleased to dwell, and through him to reconcile to himself all things, whether on earth or in heaven, making peace by the blood of his cross. (vv. 15–20)

Jesus is over all things, and all things are for Jesus. We don't worship a mere thirtysomething, humble religious leader—we worship the Cosmic King. Jesus is unlike any other religious figure. He stands above them all. Buddhism doesn't claim that Buddha made everything or that everything exists for him. But Christianity does make that strong claim: everything was made by Jesus and for the enjoyment of Jesus, including things we can't even see, things the Hubble Space Telescope is still discovering—Jesus made them all.

> We need a big *and* accessible view of Jesus – the Lord of the cosmos who will bounce a kid on his knee and raise a friend from the dead.

Paul mentions "thrones or dominions or rulers or authorities," phrases that speak of demonic powers. Jesus made them as angels, but they fell into sin and rebellion and became demons. Why does Paul bring this up? We don't live in a dualistic universe where good and evil or God and Satan are duking it out and we'll see who wins the day. No way. Jesus is the Creator and Satan is a creation. Satan isn't an equal with Jesus, as Jehovah's Witnesses teach. Jesus created Satan and Satan will answer to Jesus. The Lord of your soul is also Lord over the satanic forces—and they shudder at him.[2]

Paul says, "All things were created *for* him." Let these four words rest on your heart: All / things / for / him. Paul's point is so

---

2. "You believe that God is one; you do well. Even the demons believe—and shudder!" (James 2:19). "What have you to do with us, Jesus of Nazareth? Have you come to destroy us? I know who you are—the Holy One of God" (Mark 1:24).

clear, you'll miss it if you don't slow down. Jupiter exists for Jesus. Incredible! Clownfish, caramel macchiatos, volcanoes, deoxyribonucleic acid—it's all his. All for his enjoyment. As Francis Schaeffer might have put it, there is no nook or cranny in the universe where Jesus doesn't say, "That's mine."

And if that isn't enough to stir you to worship Jesus of Nazareth, Paul adds another coal to the furnace: "In him all things hold together." Jesus sustains the universe. He didn't create everything and step away; he creates *and* sustains. He is involved with everything in the universe. Look at the spine of this book. The glue is sticking; it's holding the pages together—but not just because that's what glue does. Glue never *just* works. Nothing ever just does its thing. Everything does its thing because Jesus is doing his thing—he's holding all things together.

Resolve not to have small thoughts of Jesus.

Resolve not to have small thoughts of Jesus.

Toss out the lucky-rabbit-foot version of Jesus and pick up the industrial-strength, universe-creating, mankind-saving Jesus—the real Jesus.

Let's go back to that storm that Jesus hushed up. Matthew tells us that the disciples *marveled* at Jesus. They were in wonder, in amazement. Jesus' band of brothers were astonished that he pulled rank over creation. How do you feel about it? Are you too left in wonder? Jesus' awesomeness is meant to incite awe and satisfaction in the beholder. So when was the last time you sat back and marveled at Jesus? Take a gander at the spectacle that is Jesus.

Jesus rebuking the storm isn't the only piece of kindling provided for your heart to be astonished. Have you seen all the incredible feats of Christ? How about his

- virgin birth
- victorious face-off with Satan in the desert
- healing a leper with a single touch

- command over demons
- ministry to the biggest sinners in society
- healing people with only a word
- restoring life to a little dead girl
- healing two blind guys
- billowing compassion
- walk across the water
- feeding twenty thousand people with a boy's lunch
- raising Lazarus from the dead

Are you marveling yet? Need still more lighter fluid?

When you read the gospels, you begin to notice that Jesus isn't trying to fall in line with the religious practices of the day—he is telling them (and us), "I'm bigger than all that you see. I'm bigger than all that you've read and experienced." Jesus points the coordinates of ancient Jewish life toward himself. He said he was greater than the temple in Jerusalem (Matt. 12:6). He said he was in charge of the Jewish holy day of rest, the Sabbath (Matt. 12:8).

Remember Jonah? Jesus said, "Just as Jonah was three days and three nights in the belly of the great fish, so will the Son of Man be three days and three nights in the heart of the earth. The men of Nineveh will rise up at the judgment with this generation and condemn it, for they repented at the preaching of Jonah, and behold, something *greater than Jonah is here*" (Matt. 12:40–41, italics mine).

King Solomon was impressive, wiser than all get-out, but Jesus of Nazareth says, "The queen of the South will rise up at the judgment with this generation and condemn it, for she came from the ends of the earth to hear the wisdom of Solomon, and behold, something greater than Solomon is here" (Matt. 12:42).

How about Abraham, that most revered of the patriarchs? In John 8, the Jews argued with Jesus, "Are you greater than our father Abraham, who died? And the prophets died! Who do you make yourself out to be?" Jesus replied, "Your father Abraham rejoiced that he would see my day. He saw it and was glad." So the Jews said to him, "You are not yet fifty years old, and have you seen Abraham?" Jesus said to them, "Truly, truly, I say to you, before Abraham was, I am" (vv. 53, 56–58).

Referring to the prophet Daniel's vision of a highly anticipated "Son of Man," Jesus said, "I am [the Christ], and you will see the Son of Man seated at the right hand of Power, and coming with the clouds of heaven" (Mark 14:62).

The prophet Isaiah found himself in the celestial throne room, where he "saw the Lord sitting upon a throne, high and lifted up; and the train of his robe filled the temple" (Isa. 6:1). Who is the Lord whom Isaiah saw? The apostle John tells us: "Isaiah said these things because he saw [Jesus'] glory and spoke of him" (John 12:41). Isaiah saw Jesus and worshiped him.

Are *you* worshiping him yet?

Let's have one more history lesson. How about the greatest event in history—and specifically, in *your* history. How about Jesus putting himself on the cross, getting right in the path of God's wrath to pay for all your sins, releasing his life unto death, and then rising from the dead for your new life.

Are you marveling? Are you worshiping?

The gospel is C-4 to lukewarm worship.

Gospel worship means to respond in exultation over the work of Jesus Christ on your behalf, in your place, for your life. It's an explosion over the gospel, and seeing your name graven on his hands ignites it. The gospel is C-4 to lukewarm worship. Gospel-centered worship echoes the once-doubting Thomas: "My Lord and my God!" (John 20:28). I want my worship to sound like *that*. I'll bet you do too.

If you are puttering about with your astonishment tank on empty, seek the Lord by soaking in the gospel. Seek the Spirit. Ask him to do this work on your heart. Only the Spirit can make you marvel. Marinate yourself in gospel truth and wait till the Spirit lights the wick.

Are you marveling at Jesus?

What especially blows you away about Jesus?

Will you pray for astonishment until it comes to you?

May you all marvel at our Messiah and experience an unprecedented excitement over the gospel.

Great are the works of the LORD, studied
by all who delight in them.

PSALM 111:2

CHAPTER 4

Worship Is War

Let the word of Christ dwell in you richly, teaching and admonishing one another in all wisdom, singing psalms and hymns and spiritual songs, with thankfulness in your hearts to God.

COLOSSIANS 3:16

Worship is always more than singing a song—but it's also not less. When we think about gospel worship, we've made a great move in the right direction: Worship is a lifestyle. The spirit-and-truth nature of worship is way more than a Sunday gathering. But as we move in the right direction, let's not forget that worship *is* singing too. It's easy, especially for theologically minded men who think they are too masculine for such stuff, to neglect singing to God. A Jesus-exalting life involves the vocal cords. There is a cosmic nature about our church singing. We need a great, gospel-centric view of our worship gatherings. I remember the Sunday that taught me this like it was yesterday.

> **A Jesus-exalting life involves the vocal cords.**

Only one more song before I was up to preach. I felt prayed-up. Ready. But then a sense of uneasiness came over me. As the first verse began to roll, I prayed, "Lord, help me. Move in your people. May you be glorified. I know the principalities and powers are against us in this place. They are looking for gospel seeds to steal. The enemy is prowling against me and your bride this day. Help us, Lord. One little word from you is all we need."

58

The forces of evil were more real to me in that moment than they had been all week (Eph. 6:12). It was then I realized that there was a snake in lion's clothing slithering through our church (1 Peter 5:8). We were going into battle. I looked to the words of "In Christ Alone" on the screen and joined the church in singing about a Roman cross and an empty grave. The gathered saints of a risen Galilean, the King of kings, were singing, exalting, and enjoying the gospel of the kingdom. As we sang the beautiful truths of the gospel, we were doing more than reciting words. This was no mere singing—pagans can sing. We were engaging in exaltational exorcism. We were pushing back the darkness around us in our minds, in our hearts, and in the air.

Cosmic battles are waged in our little churches. Things may appear quiet, neat, and orderly to our eyes, but there are powers over this present darkness, spiritual forces that are tempting, distracting, and condemning—even while we shake hands, hug, sip coffee, and take sermon notes. They want Mrs. Jones to be so wrecked by her sin that she wouldn't dare look to Jesus and believe that she's forgiven. Demons swirl around that teenager in the back row, hoping he won't confess his porn addiction to his youth leader—and especially not his parents.

Something nuclear happens when we sing the glories of Christ. We are wielding weapons-grade gospel power to tear down strongholds and cast out every word raised against the word of our Messiah, and we fall down before our Lord and follow him. "For the weapons of our warfare are not of the flesh but have divine power to destroy strongholds. We destroy arguments and every lofty opinion raised against the knowledge of God, and take every thought captive to obey Christ" (2 Cor. 10:4–5).

Satan isn't terrified of our electric guitars, live drums, or fancy-schmancy services. But when redeemed sinners exalt the triune God and exult in Jesus of Nazareth, that's the moment when demons shriek and whimper back to the darkness from which they came.

When we sing the truths of the gospel, we aren't the only ones being reminded of the victory at Calvary—the satanic powers are freshly reminded that Jesus is Lord, not Lucifer. They follow a loser.

Jesus won. Therefore, Jesus holds us; sin doesn't. Our flesh can't boss us around anymore because Jesus isn't laid up in a tomb. He stands in victory, so we stand in victory. It was on a bloody hill outside of Jerusalem that God "disarmed the rulers and authorities and put them to open shame, by triumphing over them in him [Jesus]" (Col. 2:15). Jesus has not only conquered Satan, but he has made a spectacle of him as well.

When the army of Christ assembles in high school cafeterias, warehouses, and rooms filled with theater chairs, and under thatched roofs, these buildings are more like barracks. We gather to be filled by the Spirit of the King, refreshed by his Word, and then we march back out into enemy-occupied territory, singing in unison the battle hymn of the kingdom: "God so loved the world, that he gave his only Son, that whoever believes in him should not perish but have eternal life" (John 3:16).

> Our songs, laced with gospel truth, sung in faith, are anti–air missile defense systems against the flaming darts of the Evil One.

Our songs, laced with gospel truth, sung in faith, are anti–air missile defense systems against the flaming darts of the Evil One (Eph. 6:16). Heaven rejoices and Satan watches on in horror. No power of hell can pluck us from Christ's hand. "No power of hell, Satan. Do you hear us? You and all your rotten might are no match for our Jesus."

When you sing at your church, are you actually singing or just moseying along? If you stand on Sundays dull-eyed and dragging your vocal cords on the floor, then wake up to the realness of Christ, his blood, your enemy, and victory in Jesus. This is why I advocate for loud singing (Zeph. 3:14–15). War isn't quiet. No soldier mumbles on the battlefield—and especially not at the victory party.

Belt out the glory of Christ. And know that our Champion sings loudly over us (Zeph. 3:17).

Gospel worship is hearts and vocal cords honed in on life being restored to Christ's lifeless body three days after he died, and it is remembering that Calvary happened to us too. In Paul's words, "I have been crucified with Christ. It is no longer I who live, but Christ who lives in me. And the life I now live in the flesh I live by faith in the Son of God, who loved me and gave himself for me" (Gal. 2:20). The Dark Snake lost his grip on us when Jesus gave up his life and came back from the dead, because Jesus brought us with him (Eph. 4:8). In him we too lost our lives and got them back. We died on that cross. Then we rose from the grave. We are new creations (2 Cor. 5:17). We are more than conquerors (Rom. 8:37)—and the fallen angels hate it and don't want us to know it or enjoy it. But we stand in the power of Christ.

Church singing hacks away at the unrealities we've bought into during the week. A part of spiritual warfare is cutting the heads off of lies with the sharp edge of truth. Such warfare is vital. Satan's forces work in tandem with our flesh, and without our noticing it, we start to believe that maybe we have sinned too big or too much this week, and we hang our heads and drag our knuckles on the Lord's Day. We think, "Maybe this sin is, you know, just the way it's going to be." That's all anti-gospel. That thinking didn't come from the throne but from below. We tear down that stronghold—"There is . . . no condemnation for those who are in Christ Jesus" (Rom. 8:1)—and sing.

Some people endure the time of corporate singing just so they can get to the sermon. Among the many dumb things to do in church, that's one of the big ones. You may not like the style of music, but that doesn't matter. If God wanted one style of music, or even the songs done in a certain way, we'd have sheet music instead of maps in the back of our Bibles. God commands us to sing, "Sing praises to the LORD, O you his saints, and give thanks to his holy name" (Ps. 30:4). And it might be that during those songs, we are being made ready to hear the preached Word of Christ. Singing readies us for the sermon.

The belt of truth is being tightened; we remember the righteousness of Christ as our breastplate; the gospel shoes are being laced up; and as we raise our hands in praise, we lift up the shield of faith and block the darts of the Serpent (Eph. 6:13–17). We are confident in the helmet of salvation, and we wield the sword of the Spirit through our songs. And it is in those verses and hymns, those gospel songs, that the Spirit gives us the spiritual gift of street fighting. Believe and sing; sing and believe. You are in the middle of a war. Look at the words, take them in, believe them, and let them soar into the air. Lift up the shield of faith by lifting up your voice. And sing loudly. Maybe God will use your singing to help a brother or sister look away from lies, cheap thrills, and temptations. Yours may be the voice that inspires someone to lift his or her droopy hands and dwell on Christ (Col. 3:16).

Believe and sing; sing and believe. You are in the middle of a war.

If you are a pastor or worship leader, lead us to the gospel waters. Help us hear our God's generous invitation:

> Come, everyone who thirsts,
>   come to the waters;
> and he who has no money,
>   come, buy and eat!
> Come, buy wine and milk
>   without money and without price. (Isa. 55:1)

Choose songs that are jam-packed with gospel truth. "His glories now we sing"; is your church singing about God's glories or a bunch of goofiness? Are we singing about a solid rock of truth or soggy love? If we aren't singing about the cross and the empty tomb, then what are we singing about? God's love? First John 3:16 much?[1] Take

---

1. "By this we know love, that he laid down his life for us" (1 John 3:16).

us to Jerusalem, show us Golgotha and that empty grave, and then point us to the clouds that will be rolled back like a scroll.

Martin Luther knew this kingdom warfare theme. In his powerful hymn, "A Mighty Fortress Is Our God" (1529), he sings,

> For still our ancient foe
> doth seek to work us woe;
> his craft and power are great,
> and armed with cruel hate,
> on earth is not his equal.

He knew our Enemy and his work against us. Luther's conclusion?

> And though this world, with devils filled,
> should threaten to undo us;
> we will not fear, for God hath willed
> his truth to triumph through us.
>
> The prince of darkness grim,
> we tremble not for him;
> his rage we can endure,
> for lo, his doom is sure;
> one little word shall fell him.

One word from Christ, just one, that's all. One truth—*the* truth. Like Tolkien's elvish waybread, one gospel crumb is enough to sustain the whole church for a whole lifetime. For a whole eternity.

May we sing the good song of the good news. Fight the good fight of the faith! We are in a war, after all.

Be exalted, O LORD, in your strength!
We will sing and praise your power.

PSALM 21:13

CHAPTER 5

Gospel Eye Candy

Finally, my brothers, rejoice in the Lord. To write the same things to you is no trouble to me and is safe for you.

<small>PHILIPPIANS 3:1</small>

I have a love-hate relationship with the news. No matter the network, they beat stories to death. They rerun us into a news coma. If I had to pick between listening to the same coverage of the same story with the same points all day long or the same Nickelback song, my head might go volcanic. News gets old when it ceases to be *new* news. Stories have a shelf life; their relevance wanes.

The sad reality is that we often treat the good news this way. We would never say that the gospel has lost its relevance, but we live that way more than we'd care to admit. Does hearing the gospel ever get old? We know the church answer: No, never. But what's the honest answer? Are we bored by the gospel? This is too serious to ignore.

The Lord tells us, "Keep my commandments and live; keep my teaching as the apple of your eye" (Prov. 7:2). The "apple of your eye" is a love so strong that your heart hones in and will not look away. What twinkles in your eyes? What do you fixate on? Is God's teaching the apple of your eye? How does the Bible rank in your life?

Gospel-centered people consume the Bible voraciously, like the prophet Jeremiah: "Your words were found, and I *ate* them, and your words became to me a joy and the delight of my heart" (Jer. 15:16, italics mine). You might be thinking, "Why does it matter if the Bible is my heart's delight? I thought this book was about Jesus?" Yes. Exactly. Once we see what the Bible is actually all about—the glory of God in the work of his Son—our heart explodes in joy. Worship is echoed from the Word. The heart exults in the exaltation of God. Christians love the Bible not simply for the facts and truths we find, but because the Bible ushers us into the worship of God. We learn more about God. We see God's awesome love and power. We see the great story of God and his love for rebels. We are thrown at the feet of God and humbled by his grace. And there in the words of God we discover and worship the Word of God—Jesus Christ.

When the Lord says, "Keep my teaching as the apple of your eye," he also means, "Keep *me* as the apple of your eye." How does Jesus rank in your life? If the Bible is the apple of your eye, logically it should be because Jesus is the apple of your eye; a true love for the Bible stems from a Jesus obsession. When the gospel crashes into our lives, what we cherish changes. Plain and simple, Jesus takes the cake. Jesus takes the number one spot. And gospel-centered living means that we want him to stay there, so we defend our hearts against all competitors by wielding the "sword of the Spirit, which is the word of God" (Eph. 6:17).

> **When the gospel crashes into our lives, what we cherish changes.**

If Jesus' death on the cross for you has become old hat, maybe you're looking at the cross all wrong. Or maybe you have some other apples in your eye. The gospel is more than something you responded to with a prayer of faith back in yesteryear; it's for today too. The good news is always relevant. Jesus saved you back then, and he is sustaining and changing you today.

Andrew Bonar (1810–1892), a Jesus-exalting minister in Scotland, is right when he says, "The glad tidings of great joy all cluster round that Person."[1] Jesus is the essence of joy. The gospel of grace is more vital than world news, politics, and whatever the day holds.

---

1. Andrew Bonar, *The Person of Christ* (1858 edition; Kindle edition, 2010).

Soon you will be significantly tempted if you haven't been already. In that blip, sin is going to look really good. How will you stand? White-knuckle your way through? How many potholes and cliffs can you avoid with that style of sanctification? A few. But you will eventually crash. Satan will try to make you feel worthless. He'll attack you with your past. His minions will pester you about your lack of personal growth. And your flesh—my goodness, the flesh! It will try to compare you to other Christians.

What are you going to do? What *should* you do? Where are your eyes looking?

Fixate on the gospel of grace. The power of Christ—the same power that raised Jesus from the dead—now lives in you. Recall what the gospel says about you: You are new, forgiven, freed, and accepted. God is for you, not against you. Flood your heart with gospel truths and Satan will scram. Preach the gospel to yourself. Keep dropping the high-voltage cable of the gospel on your heart and it will spark soon enough. It's the power of God.[2]

> **Recall what the gospel says about you: You are new, forgiven, freed, and accepted.**

Here's one simple yet powerful thing you can do: take John 3:16 and soak your heart in it. Yes, John 3:16: "For God so loved the world, that he gave his only Son, that whoever believes in him should not perish but have eternal life." However many times you've read, heard, or said that verse, it's safe for you to hear it again and again. Familiarity shouldn't breed apathy: this verse sparks fire! Let your heart hang on each word; there is enough to chew on for hours, years, a lifetime—even eternity. Use the most famous "salvation verse" in the Bible as a powerful weapon for your sanctification. Use it to make an all-out assault on indifference.

---

2. "I am not ashamed of the gospel, for it is the power of God for salvation to everyone who believes, to the Jew first and also to the Greek" (Rom. 1:16).

If you want to enjoy the Word—and enjoy Jesus—go pick some eye apples from the Scriptures. Gospel-hungry Christians want the glory of Jesus Christ to be their eye apples, and the best place in the universe to find such fruit is in the Book of Books. God's mighty acts, prophecies and promises, gospel shadows and types, the cross, the Lamb, the empty tomb, the Spirit—if you don't experience these as delicacies for the soul, then say to God, "Open my eyes, that I may behold wondrous things out of your law" (Ps. 119:18). Eye apples grow wild throughout the Scriptures. Dig in.

Treasure the Bible because you treasure Christ. And if your eyes and heart feast on other things—change your diet. Ask God to transform your taste buds.[3] Take on a steady diet of God's Word and trust that you will "taste and see that the LORD is good" (Ps. 34:8).

May you attack apathy with the power of the gospel. May God's love bring fire to your soul.

Incline your ear, and come to me;
hear, that your soul may live.

ISAIAH 55:3

---

3. "Incline my heart to your testimonies, and not to selfish gain!" (Ps. 119:36).

CHAPTER 6

Jesus Ignites Inexpressible Joy

*Though you have not seen him, you love
him. Though you do not now see him,
you believe in him and rejoice with joy that
is inexpressible and filled with glory.*

1 PETER 1:8

We've all had our fair share of letdowns. Raved-over restaurants fall flat. Hyped movies turn out to be snoozers. And in June 2013, scores of bird-watchers in the United Kingdom met with utter disappointment. Some even wept. If you are a bird enthusiast (which I'm not; birds are too shifty for my liking), I can't imagine a more crushing day.

A lone white-throated needletail, the world's fastest bird in level flight, was reported in the small Scottish town of Tarbert on the Isle of Harris. In 170 years, this rare bird had made only eight showings in the UK. With twenty-two years gone by since the last sighting, this occasion was sure to delight. Across Britain, birders set off on a pilgrimage, hoping to catch a glimpse of the needletail in all its glory and maybe even Instagram a few shots.

The first group watched the creature as it skimmed through the air. Many more birders were on their way—but in vain. With cameras snapping and fans gawking, suddenly the rare white-throated needletail became even rarer when its British representative flew into a wind turbine before the eyes of horrified spectators. A quick, quiet exit. Just like that. Talk about a party fowl.[1]

Bummer. Especially for the bird, but a bummer all around.

Expectations of beholding a majestic and rare creature got dashed in a moment. No one saw what they hoped for, and what observers did see, they wished they could have un-seen. A total letdown.

Maybe you feel like those birders when it comes to your experience of Christianity. Every Sunday you hear the music, but nothing happens in your heart. You sing, but you know that a parrot could produce the same words. You leave disappointed. You try to read the Bible, but the verses seem to keep hitting the turbines whirling in your head. *Gadonk!* There went that verse—for the fourth time.

We all want to experience real, vibrant, powerful Christianity. Maybe you long for a smidge of needletail-birder-like enthusiasm for Jesus. I'll bet you're not alone. So how do we get to the kind of worship that 1 Peter 1:8 talks about, in which we "rejoice with joy that is inexpressible"?

> Our worship gets energized when we remember the awesomeness of Jesus, the Father, the Spirit, and the gospel of the kingdom.

The answer is not as complicated as we think.

Our worship gets energized when we remember the awesomeness of Jesus, the Father, the Spirit, and the gospel of the kingdom. It's that simple.

Our worship, our responding to God, can seem soggy because we've forgotten the atomic power of grace. When our attention gets locked on the things of earth, and we fail to remember who is

---

1. Melanie Hall, "Twitchers Flocking to See Rare Bird Saw It Killed by Wind Turbine," *The Telegraph*, June 27, 2013, http://www.telegraph.co.uk /earth/environment/10146081/Twitchers-flocking-to-see-rare-bird-saw-it-killed -by-wind-turbine.html.

sitting on the throne, then we become nearsighted to the point of blindness, forgetting that we've been cleansed from our former sins (2 Peter 1:9).

We need a fresh dose of gospel truth about the man from Nazareth who rules the universe. Get *that* and thankfulness will begin to flow—and thankfulness is the spark plug for worshiping God. Be thankful! Not only do you have good things in life such as a home and food, but your sins are paid for, you're new, you're saved, and you're greatly loved by God! When was the last time you thanked him for these eternal realities? Tell him you are thankful. Respond to his gospel. Put its corrective lenses back on your nearsighted eyes and look to a bloody hill outside of Jerusalem. Look to Jesus' cross and empty tomb.

The old, old story never gets old. It's what we always need. Can we ever grow tired of God's love? Never. It's too big, too deep. Is there a more hulking display of God's love than the gospel? John 3:16 says no. Don't hem in the sovereign God's love for little ol' you. God's love shines in the gospel and it echoes in all of life—even in the death of a white-throated needletail.

Remember what Jesus said about birds? "Not one of them will fall to the ground apart from your Father. But even the hairs of your head are all numbered. Fear not, therefore; you are of more value than many sparrows" (Matt. 10:29–31). Christian, you are more precious to God than a thousand white-throated needletails. The Son of God left heaven for your joy; Jesus Christ died for your joy; the God-man from Nazareth rose for your joy; the Alpha and Omega sits on the throne, alive and well, for your joy—your joy *in him*.

When we truly see the glories of the gospel, we won't be the same—and neither will our worship. It will be real. Authentic. Grace-driven. Our worship will take on the flair that Peter describes in this chapter's key verse: it will be filled with glory.

Gospel worship has a certain zest to it, a nuance that is much more than simply digging a catchy melody or guitar riff. A gospel-centered heart dances to the beat of a different exegesis. It looks for a crucified Galilean; it listens for echoes of "It is finished!" Many claim that if churches aren't giving eye-popping visuals, people will be lumps in the pew; the gospel, however, gives a different perspective. The gospel doesn't need to be dressed up to inspire worship; it just needs to be seen with the eyes of the heart. Faith in Jesus ignites worship. The person and work of Jesus will set your heart ablaze for him.

> The gospel doesn't need to be dressed up to inspire worship; it just needs to be seen with the eyes of the heart.

Peter declares a startling truth about every Christian: we have never seen Jesus, but we sure love him! Peter speaks with such enthusiasm that he nearly contradicts himself, on purpose, to reveal the kind of ultra-delighting in Christ the gospel brings.

"Rejoice with joy that is inexpressible"—what in the world? How can we express what is inexpressible? Peter isn't being cute, and you can be sure he isn't contradicting himself. He is drawing us into gospel-centered worship. Worship grounded on the gospel runs deeper than words: it's about a heart on fire. When a Christian responds to the gospel by exalting God in song, prayer, shouts of praise, Scripture, holy silence, and so on, and none of it gets old, that's joy inexpressible. That kind of worship—gospel worship—doesn't have a shelf life. There is always more to sing about, more glories to exult over, more of Jesus to enjoy.

Inexpressible joy means that the river never dries up. It perpetually flows with thankfulness and praise unto God. Its tributaries of faith and life experience all meet up and cause us to exult, "He has caused us to be born again to a living hope through the resurrection of Jesus Christ from the dead" (1 Peter 1:3).

Though we don't see Jesus, we love him because we know what he did for us and who he is. We know what happened at that blood-soaked hill called Calvary. We know why nails pierced his skin. We know why he died—to pay for our sins and bring us back to God.[2] And we know there is an empty tomb in a garden in Jerusalem. That's gospel worship.

Can you imagine what it will be like when we finally see him? My tear ducts flip on at the thought. Christian, that day is coming. We will see our best friend. Nail-pierced hands will welcome us home. I seriously doubt we will be disappointed. I'm confident that all of our expectations will be exceeded, more than we could ever imagine.[3]

When the gospel burrows deep into your heart, your joy will be inexpressible, uncontainable, and completely understandable—because Jesus is incredible.

How excited are you about Jesus?

Do you love him?

Does this chapter's key verse, 1 Peter 1:8, describe your worship of Jesus?

What keeps you from this kind of worship?

May you rejoice today with joy that is inexpressible over the glory of the gospel in the face of Jesus Christ!

"These things I have spoken to you, that my joy may be in you, and that your joy may be full."

JOHN 15:11

---

2. "For Christ also suffered once for sins, the righteous for the unrighteous, that he might bring us to God, being put to death in the flesh but made alive in the spirit" (1 Peter 3:18).

3. "Now to him who is able to do far more abundantly than all that we ask or think . . ." (Eph. 3:20).

CHAPTER 7

The King Jesus Bible

"You search the Scriptures because you think
that in them you have eternal life; and it is
they that bear witness about me."

JOHN 5:39

There is glory all around us, and we are missing it.

Have you heard the story about the world-famous violinist who played for free in the New York subway, and no one cared?

Or how about Banksy? He is one of our day's most sought-after painters, creating street art that is worth millions. One Saturday in New York City's Central Park, Banksy set up a non-eye-popping stall and began to sell his super-sought-after work. During the course of the day, only three people bought prints from the old man watching over the stall, which was subtly labeled "Spray Art." One lady bought two small canvases and bargained her way into getting a 50 percent discount. (Careful there, kids—each one of those is worth a year's college tuition!) A young woman bought a larger canvas for regular price. Some lucky guy from Chicago bought four for his new house. He just wanted "something for the walls."

That day, the *Guardian* estimates, Banksy sold about $225,000 worth of art for just $420. (The entire stall was probably holding over $1 million worth of canvases.)[1] The hottest thing in art was

---

1. Adam Clark Estes, "Banksy Sold $225,000 Worth of Art at a Central Park Stall for $420," Gizmodo, October 14, 2013, http://gizmodo.com/banksy-sold-225-000-worth-of-art-at-a-central-park-sta-1444833251?utm_source=recirculation.

totally ignored. No one recognized the immense value on display right before their eyes.

Are we any different? How many of us are completely clueless to the true awesomeness of Jesus that is right in front of us? We can be honest here. We've probably all been bored by the Bible at some point. My hand is raised too. For many a Sunday morning, I used my thick study Bible as a jack. It propped my arm up just enough, to help me catch a good nap during the sermon.

What changed? How did I go from that to being a pastor, a preacher of the Bible, and the author of this book? My eyes got opened to what the Bible is all about—or should I say, to *whom* the Bible is all about: Jesus.

> **When we read the Bible, we aren't just reading a book – we are meeting with a person.**

If the Bible is merely a dusty collection of stories, facts, data, and one-liners that make us feel bad, then of course we won't be drawn to it. And if the Bible isn't about Jesus, then we might as well take up Judaism or Islam. But the Bible *is* about Jesus. It's all about our Savior. When we read the Bible, we aren't just reading a book—we are meeting with a person: the second person of the Trinity, the eternal Son of God, the God-man and our friend, Jesus of Nazareth.

For many, Jesus might seem impersonal, distant, or just fuzzy. If that is your view of him, then you won't be drawn to him or his Word. I encourage you to read the gospels and truly *see* Jesus, and discover how the entire Bible is about him.

In John 5:39, Jesus tells the Scripture-loving Pharisees that they are missing the point. There is a sinful way to love the Bible, and the Pharisees were guilty of it. They loved the Scriptures, but they didn't love God because they didn't love Jesus. Don't read the Bible like they did. The Pharisees loved the frills of religion, but it got them nothing. We need to keep that in mind. Zeal for spirituality, Christian hoopla, and the latest jargon doesn't make us gospel-centered, and a generic love for the Bible doesn't equal a genuine love for God. One can know all kinds of Bible verses and still miss the point of the Bible.

The Pharisees were the original Old Testament scholars, yet look at what Jesus said to them: "You search the Scriptures because you think that in them you have eternal life; and *it is they that bear witness about me*, yet you refuse to come to me that you may have life. . . . Do not think that I will accuse you to the Father. There is one who accuses you: Moses, on whom you have set your hope. For if you believed Moses, you would believe me; for *he wrote of me*" (John 5:39–40, 45–46, italics mine).

Moses wrote about Jesus. They all wrote about Jesus. All 804,566 words in the English Bible[2] lead us to one word: Jesus. Front to back, top to bottom, it's all Jesus all the time.

- Genesis to Deuteronomy is the foundation for Jesus.
- Joshua to Esther is the preparation for Jesus.
- Job to Song of Solomon is the longing for Jesus.
- Isaiah to Malachi is the expectation of Jesus.[3]
- Matthew to John is the life and ministry of Jesus.
- Acts is the continued work and spreading of the fame of Jesus and the growth of his church.
- Romans to Jude is about living for Jesus.
- Revelation is about the return, reign, and rule of Jesus.

It's all about Jesus. It's all for Jesus. When you sit with an open Bible, you should set out to meet with Jesus, to worship Jesus. The

---

2. Numbers are from the English Standard Version. The stats on other translations can be found at: http://www.crossway.org/blog/2007/11/bible-text-stats/.

3. My Christocentric Old Testament summary is adapted from Norman L. Geisler, *A Popular Survey of the Old Testament* (Grand Rapids: Baker, 1977), 21–22.

> **The Holy Spirit's goal in the Word is to show you Jesus so you can behold his glory and live in response to his radiance.**

Holy Spirit's goal in the Word is to show you Jesus so you can behold his glory and live in response to his radiance.

The Bible is filled with neon signs that beam "Jesus." These are the prophecies. There are also shadows, or *typologies*, that whisper "Jesus." What is a typology? According to Old Testament professor David Murray, "Basically [typology] means 'picture-ology.' It's a kind of visual theology. God pictured the truth to preach the truth."[4]

For example, the New Testament says that Jesus is the Creator of everything, "for by him all things were created, in heaven and on earth, visible and invisible, whether thrones or dominions or rulers or authorities—all things were created through him and for him" (Col. 1:16). That's a mind-blowing, soul-stirring neon sign. Dr. Murray helps us hear the whispers of creation:

> Have you ever thought about the incredible imagination and inventiveness behind the created world and asked why? Why did our Redeemer go to such lengths to provide us with such a varied and diverse world? Partly the reason was that He had an eye to using these things, animals, materials, and so on to teach sinners the way of salvation. He was preparing visual aids for future use.
>
> He created sheep so He could teach sinners about how He is the Good Shepherd. He created birds to help His redeemed people live less anxious lives. He created camels to teach how hard it is for those who

---

4. David Murray, *Jesus on Every Page: 10 Simple Ways to Seek and Find Christ in the Old Testament* (Nashville: Nelson, 2013), 136.

trust in riches to enter heaven. He created lilies and roses so He could compare Himself with them. He created water to explain how He refreshes and revives the thirsty.[5]

Creation sings the glory of Jesus. The wind is an illustration of the Spirit and what happens when we are born again (John 3:8). Lions remind us of the Lion of Judah and tell us something about his character; lambs show us the Lamb of God who takes away the sins of the world (John 1:29). Even the sweetness of a freshly cut pineapple from Hawaii is a sermon: "Taste and see that the Lord is good" (Ps. 34:8). When we read the Bible christologically, with Jesus at the center, we see the universe christologically as well.

> Even the sweetness of a freshly cut pineapple from Hawaii is a sermon: "Taste and see that the Lord is good" (Ps. 34:8).

We must grasp that the Old Testament is as much about Jesus as the New Testament is. Consider the shadowy whispers of Old Testament accounts. Noah and the ark is a good example. It's a powerful story. But Noah isn't the perfect hero we need. After he left the arky arky, Noah had himself a little too much to drinky drinky. Fortunately, the story doesn't end with Noah. It shows us something greater: God's provision for us to escape his judgment. Noah, his family, and the animals all enter the ark, all because of faith in God's word. The ark protected Noah—he didn't feel a drop of God's wrath because the ark took it for him. The ark is a shadow of Jesus, who took God's wrath upon himself. Noah and the ark is more than a great story—it's a gospel story, a picture of Jesus standing in our place.

The book of Proverbs provides powerful wisdom for life. We

---

5. Ibid., 47.

don't have to wonder, "What would Jesus do?" Proverbs answers that question. Jesus is the proverbial wise man. Jesus lived the Proverbs for us and empowers us to live them too. He is our wisdom.[6]

Tim Keller helps us see the shadows of Jesus in the Old Testament when he says:

> Jesus is the true and better Adam who passed the test in the garden and whose obedience is imputed to us.
>
> Jesus is the true and better Abel who, though innocently slain, has blood now that cries out, not for our condemnation, but for acquittal.
>
> Jesus is the true and better Abraham who answered the call of God to leave all the comfortable and familiar and go out into the void not knowing whither he went to create a new people of God.
>
> Jesus is the true and better Isaac who was not just offered up by his father on the mount but was truly sacrificed for us. And when God said to Abraham, "Now I know you love me because you did not withhold your son, your only son whom you love from me," now we can look at God taking his son up the mountain and sacrificing him and say, "Now we know that you love us because you did not withhold your son, your only son, whom you love from us."
>
> Jesus is the true and better Jacob who wrestled and took the blow of justice we deserved, so we, like Jacob, only receive the wounds of grace to wake us up and discipline us.
>
> Jesus is the true and better Joseph who, at the

---

6. "But to those who are called, both Jews and Greeks, Christ [is] the power of God and the wisdom of God. . . . And because of [God] you are in Christ Jesus, who became to us wisdom from God, righteousness and sanctification and redemption" (1 Cor. 1:24, 30).

right hand of the king, forgives those who betrayed and sold him and uses his new power to save them.

Jesus is the true and better Moses who stands in the gap between the people and the Lord and who mediates a new covenant.

Jesus is the true and better Rock of Moses who, struck with the rod of God's justice, now gives us water in the desert.

Jesus is the true and better Job, the truly innocent sufferer, who then intercedes for and saves his stupid friends.

Jesus is the true and better David whose victory becomes his people's victory, though they never lifted a stone to accomplish it themselves.

Jesus is the true and better Esther who didn't just risk leaving an earthly palace but lost the ultimate and heavenly one, who didn't just risk his life, but gave his life to save his people.

Jesus is the true and better Jonah who was cast out into the storm so that we could be brought in.

Jesus is the real Rock of Moses, the real Passover Lamb, innocent, perfect, helpless, slain so the angel of death will pass over us. He's the true temple, the true prophet, the true priest, the true king, the true sacrifice, the true lamb, the true light, the true bread.

The Bible's really not about you—it's about him.[7]

Hallelujah!

Gospel-driven saints love the Bible because it's about their first

---

7. Justin Taylor, "Keller: Gospel-Centered Ministry," The Gospel Coalition, May 23, 2007, http://thegospelcoalition.org/blogs/justintaylor/2007/05/23/keller-gospel-centered-ministry/. From a message by Timothy Keller.

love, their great God and Savior, the King of kings, the Lord of lords, the great I AM, the Lamb, the Lion—Jesus of Nazareth. We live to exult in Jesus.

May you love the Word of God, the Bible, because it gives you the Word of God, Jesus.[8]

Then he said to them, "These are my words that I spoke to you while I was still with you, that everything written about me in the Law of Moses and the Prophets and the Psalms must be fulfilled." Then he opened their minds to understand the Scriptures.

LUKE 24:44–45

---

8. "In the beginning was the Word, and the Word was with God, and the Word was God" (John 1:1). "For the word of God is living and active, sharper than any two-edged sword, piercing to the division of soul and of spirit, of joints and of marrow, and discerning the thoughts and intentions of the heart. And no creature is hidden from his sight, but all are naked and exposed to the eyes of him to whom we must give account" (Heb. 4:12–13).

CHAPTER 8

Deep and Wide Worship

We impart a secret and hidden wisdom of God,
which God decreed before the ages for our glory.

1 CORINTHIANS 2:7

I recently got into a spat with a nasty virus: 104.4-degree fever, aches, chills, the works. And while locked away from my family, I did what any sane person would do—I took to Netflix.

During my sequester, I dove into BBC's *Sherlock*. I've always been fascinated by Mr. Holmes. He has a freakishly keen ability to discern and deduce. And after he's performed one of his feats, Sherlock is known for quipping to his sidekick, "It's elementary, my dear Watson."

Elementary? Nothing Sherlock does is elementary. His skills are highly advanced. Yet he's only seeing what is already there. And that's how it is when it comes to living the Christian life. We don't need to look for some spiritual unicorn. We just need to look at what is already there.

The gospel is elementary *and* advanced. The gospel is for new and old Christians, hurting and thriving Christians, excited and ashamed Christians. We all need the same thing: a deep soak in gospel truth. In Jesus there is a fountain flowing deep and wide. It's time for us to go deep—deep into the gospel.

"Going deep" doesn't mean studying the end times or the original biblical languages. It's not about reading up on the four keys to this, that, or the other. It doesn't mean listening to hour-long sermons with three alliterated points (or no points at all), and it has nothing to do with Sunday school. Going deep means plunging into the grace of God. Paul says that in Jesus "are hidden all the treasures of wisdom and knowledge" (Col. 2:3). It doesn't get any deeper than Jesus.

Gospel teaching is deep teaching; the depths of "deep" are found in Jesus. Gospel-formed hearts are hungry to "know the love of Christ that surpasses knowledge" (Eph. 3:19). That's what we need to know more than anything: Christ's love for rascals like us. So if your pastor labors to preach the gospel, listen to him. Deeply. Intently. Prayerfully. Even if you've heard the gospel a bazillion times. It is never wrong for him to remind you of it; in fact, it's safe for you.[1]

The evangelical church is flimsy today because too many pulpits are busy scratching people's ears rather than preaching to their hearts. But Diet Gospel is no gospel. It lacks the iron and other essential nutrients your soul needs. It's chock-full of cotton candy that pleases the palate but destroys the soul's digestive track. Gospel-deficient sermons and books build churches and Christians with gummy bear spines. The gospel, on the other hand, builds courageous Christians; the book of Acts is full of them.

> **Gospel-deficient sermons and books build churches and Christians with gummy bear spines.**

Do you want to go deep? Center your life on the gospel by supergluing the glories of grace to your heart, head, and hands—daily. Recover the gospel; have a personal reformation by preaching the gospel to yourself. You are justified, you are being sanctified, and you will be glorified. You are forgiven and freed. In Christ, you are greatly loved. God has redeemed you. Jesus calls you his friend and family member. The Holy Spirit of God dwells in you, empowering you to live like Jesus for the glory of Jesus. We need Jesus for *everything*. Think about it.

---

1. "Finally, my brothers, rejoice in the Lord. To write the same things to you is no trouble to me and is safe for you" (Phil. 3:1).

How involved is Jesus in your daily life? What is he doing for you right this second? Think about your lungs. Are you making them do what they do? What about your heart? Are you forcing its beat? What about the synapses in your brain that are reading the letters on this page and forming them into words that you comprehend? What about the food you ate? Do you tell your stomach to break it down, absorb the energy and nutrients needed, and expel the rest? All of these things are occurring under the sovereign orchestration of Jesus, and apart from him you can't do a single thing. It's in him that you and I live, move, and have our being (Acts 17:28). We need Jesus every nanosecond. And the good news is that Jesus never steps away from his role at the right hand of the Father as our mediator and advocate.

But to only consider the physical or outward nature of our dependence on Jesus would be a crime against John 15:5, in which Jesus speaks of how we can't bear fruit in the Christian life apart from him. He is the vine. We are the branches. We bear fruit because we are *in* him; he grows the fruit because he is the root. We can't grow without Jesus. We can't become like Jesus without Jesus. A husband can't love his wife as Jesus loves the church without the help and power of Jesus. We can't work under human authority in a God-glorifying way, as Jesus did, without his help and power. We need Jesus in order to live the Christian life. Living in complete dependence on him *is* the Christian life.

Let's take this further, higher, and deeper into the love of Jesus. We cannot be accepted before God without him. God invites us into the kingdom because Jesus bought us full access. Jesus paid our way; he is our backstage pass into the throne room of God. We are *in* with God, because Jesus bought and brought us. We roll with him. Apart from him we got nothin'. Apart from him—we can't do anything.

It is in the vast love of Jesus, displayed on that forsaken tree, that we find the deepest truth and the fulfillment of our greatest need. As the old hymn "O the Deep, Deep Love of Jesus" (Samuel Trevor Francis, 1875) invites us to sing:

O the deep, deep love of Jesus, vast, unmeasured,
   boundless, free!
Rolling as a mighty ocean in its fullness over me!
Underneath me, all around me, is the current of Thy love
Leading onward, leading homeward to Thy glorious rest
   above!

O the deep, deep love of Jesus, spread His praise from
   shore to shore!
How He loveth, ever loveth, changeth never,
   nevermore!
How He watches o'er His loved ones, died to call them
   all His own;
How for them He intercedeth, watcheth o'er them from
   the throne!

O the deep, deep love of Jesus, love of every love the
   best!
'Tis an ocean full of blessing, 'tis a haven giving rest!
O the deep, deep love of Jesus, 'tis a heaven of heavens
   to me;
And it lifts me up to glory, for it lifts me up to Thee!

That's what's deep: divine love, vast, boundless, and free for bumbling sinners like you and me. His cross is deeper than we realize. It is deep enough to plunge through the bowels of hell and deliver the deathblow to our ancient foe. That's the love of Jesus. He kills snakes and lifts up sinners—and he'll carry us the rest of the way.

So when we want to go deep, we go gospel-deep.[2] There is noth-

---

2. Recommended reading: Jared C. Wilson, *Gospel Deeps: Reveling in the Excellencies of Jesus* (Wheaton, IL: Crossway, 2012); and John Piper, *God Is the Gospel: Meditations on God's Love as the Gift of Himself* (Wheaton, IL: Crossway, 2005).

ing deeper than the glory of Christ. The gospel has been a cosmic mystery—and now it belongs to you. Don't treat it like some dollar store, bargain bin item. As Paul says, "In [Jesus] we have redemption through his blood, the forgiveness of our trespasses, according to the riches of his grace, which he lavished upon us,

> That's the love of Jesus. He kills snakes and lifts up sinners – and he'll carry us the rest of the way.

in all wisdom and insight *making known to us the mystery of his will,* according to his purpose, which he set forth in Christ as a plan for the fullness of time, to unite all things in him, things in heaven and things on earth" (Eph. 1:7–10, italics mine).

Gospel-centeredness won't result in an imbalanced approach to the Scriptures; if anything, you'll see how the cross and the empty tomb irrigate everything in the Bible. Often, when people say that they want to go deep, what they want is to talk about end-times theology. Dig deep enough into the gospel and you will start to think rightly about the end times: Jesus is coming back for his church, which he bought with his life. The end times are all about the Alpha and Omega.[3] A Jesus-centered eschatology is more valuable than a tribulation-centered obsession. Rummage around in the gospel and you'll see how it all comes back, like metal to a magnet, to a set of nail-pierced hands and feet.

May you go deep. Or as Hebrews 12:2 says, keep looking to Jesus.

Looking to Jesus, the founder and perfecter of our faith, who for the joy that was set before him endured the cross, despising the shame, and is seated at the right hand of the throne of God.

Hebrews 12:2

---

3. "The revelation of Jesus Christ . . ." (Rev. 1:1).

CHAPTER 9

The Happiness of Grace

But he gives more grace.

JAMES 4:6

Man Loses Life Savings on Carnival Game, Wins Giant Stuffed Banana with Dreadlocks.

True story. Henry Gribbohm reported that he lost his life savings of $2,600 on a carnival game. The thirty-year-old New Hampshire dad was hoping for a day of fun with his kids in April 2013, but then something happened: he got hooked on the game. He had to win. He spent $300 in a matter of minutes, went home to grab the rest of his cash, and then lost that as well. "For once in my life I happened to become that sucker," said Gribbohm. "[I] was foolish for putting up my life savings."[1] Um, yeah.

Henry is more than just a guy who flushed $2,600 for a dreadlock-sporting banana—he is a metaphor for our souls. We all seek that moment of joy, victory, and excitement. We want true and lasting happiness. We want *life*. But we are notorious for looking in all the wrong places: money, food, drink, relationships, iThings, achievements—life's carnival games.

All of these things are fun and bring momentary gladness. But

---

1. Michael Rosenfield, "NH Man Loses Life Savings on Carnival Game," CBS Boston, April 29, 2013, http://boston.cbslocal.com/2013/04/29/nh-man -loses-life-savings-on-carnival-game/.

we need something that lasts longer, something that is forever. In Christ we are given a never-ending joy, because there is no end to him. There is no end to his love, no shortage of his power, and no limited edition of his grace.

You will never find God's tank of grace on "E." Never. At our most desperate moment, when we think we've reached the last drop of God's love and he couldn't possibly be gracious again toward *that* sin—sure enough, God gives more grace. I love these words from Ray Ortlund in a sermon he preached on Psalm 85, titled "God Gives New Beginnings": "What does God give to those who have squandered his grace? He gives more grace!"[2] Yes! Amen! Thank you, Lord!

> **We will never arrive at the fiscal cliff of grace.**

God's grace toward us cannot be extinguished. We will never arrive at the fiscal cliff of grace. When—not if—we've mismanaged his grace, what does God draw us back with? More grace. When we have spit on the grace of God, what is it that comforts us yet again? Grace, grace, grace. It's all grace, like the old hymn croons:

> Marvelous grace of our loving Lord,
> Grace that exceeds our sin and our guilt!
> Yonder on Calvary's mount outpoured,
> There where the blood of the Lamb was spilt.
>
> Grace, grace, God's grace,
> Grace that will pardon and cleanse within;
> Grace, grace, God's grace,
> Grace that is greater than all our sin.
>   (Julia Johnston, 1911)

---

2. Ray Ortlund, "God Gives New Beginnings," sermon, March 27, 2011, https://www.covlife.org/resources/3856913-God_Gives_New_Beginnings.

Psalm 32:1 says, "Blessed is the one whose transgression is forgiven, whose sin is covered." The word *blessed* in Hebrew literally means "How happy!" Biblical blessedness is nothing short of euphoria. The truly blessed person is on cloud nine. And you only get this happy because your sins have been forgiven. Totally forgiven. Forever forgiven. Happiness comes with the covering of your sins. It's a package deal. "Covering" means that the man who is dead-broke gets his bill paid in full. The gospel truth is that Jesus took care of your sins for you. God himself settled the account. If you are a Christian, God the Son covered all of your sins with his very own blood. Your past, present, and future failings were baptized into his blood, and they've all been forgiven. Every last one. Paid for.

Biblical happiness is totally circumstantial: Do I believe my sins are paid for or not? Is Jesus alive or not? When those truths grab you, heaven's joy—Jesus himself—becomes your joy. Therefore gospel-centered people glow. "Those who look to him are radiant, and their faces shall never be ashamed" (Ps. 34:5). The feeling of being forgiven amps up our gladness, and gloom leaves the face.[3]

If you aren't experiencing the happiness of God's forgiveness described in Psalm 32:1, then know that God wants you to *feel* it. God wants you to experience the grand happiness he purchased with Jesus' blood. Forgiveness and happiness go hand in hand. They are inseparable. Forgiveness from God lasts forever. He doesn't back-pedal on his promise that whoever believes in Jesus will not perish but have eternal life. So if your happiness is gone, then your remembrance of being forgiven left first.

Gospel-centered living is happy living. So what's obstructing your joy? The gospel is like Drano for all that clogs up glad hearts. Go to Calvary and sit awhile. Rejoice and be glad, for you've been

---

3. "A glad heart makes a cheerful face, but by sorrow of heart the spirit is crushed" (Prov. 15:13).

forgiven. God brought you into his home and calls you his own. Sit at the cross and wait till joy returns. The biggest sinner you know, the one in the mirror, is totally forgiven because of Jesus. And you will *always* be forgiven because of Jesus.

> **You have never read enough, prayed enough, or obeyed enough to get his grace – that's what makes it grace.**

You have never read enough, prayed enough, or obeyed enough to get his grace—that's what makes it grace. We've sinned enough. We've been desperate enough.

> For we ourselves were once foolish, disobedient, led astray, slaves to various passions and pleasures, passing our days in malice and envy, hated by others and hating one another. But when the goodness and loving kindness of God our Savior appeared, he saved us, not because of works done by us in righteousness, but according to his own mercy, by the washing of regeneration and renewal of the Holy Spirit, whom he poured out on us richly through Jesus Christ our Savior, so that being justified by his grace we might become heirs according to the hope of eternal life. (Titus 3:3–7)

Oh, how sinful! How ridiculous, how shameful our condition—and how marvelous is the goodness and sin-crushing kindness of the Lord Jesus! It doesn't make us cower in the corner. No, it invites us to run freely—to sprint and spin through the fenceless pasture of grace. Enjoy it! Take it in! He gives more grace. And here's why that grace won't run out:

> For the grace of God has appeared, bringing salvation for all people, training us to renounce ungodliness

> and worldly passions, and to live self-controlled, upright, and godly lives in the present age, waiting for our blessed hope, the appearing of the glory of our great God and Savior Jesus Christ, who gave himself for us to redeem us from all lawlessness and to purify for himself a people for his own possession who are zealous for good works. (Titus 2:11–14)

It wasn't a mere concept that "appeared, bringing salvation"—it was a person. Jesus did it! Grace isn't some nebulous force intended to give us warm fuzzies toward God. Grace is one of Jesus' nicknames. When God gives us more grace, he gives us more of himself, more of Jesus. But it's not like he's been holding out on us; that's not what James 4:6 implies when it says that "he gives more grace." Two verses later, James says, "He will draw near to you." The whole context of James 4 is about Christians who are embroiled in worldliness. James comforts them by saying, "He gives more grace. . . . He will draw near to you."

Like the Prodigal Son being hugged by his father, we'll *feel* God's grace.

Like the Prodigal Son being hugged by his father, we'll *feel* God's grace. We will sense his kindness, omni-goodness, and all-around love. Repentance brings a refreshment of grace. It's thrilling to the last drop—which will never arrive, because there is no end to God's grace. Jesus drank from the cup of wrath so we could drink from the bottomless cup of blessing. The Lord's Supper doesn't have a limited stock; his body and blood, reflected in the bread and the cup, are perpetually available for your refreshment in grace.

Remembering Jesus through the bread and the cup is a sacred and joyous duty. How joyous are you when it's time to eat the holy meal? The New Testament doesn't say a word about dimming the lights, playing a soft and slow ballad, and having everyone sit with heads bowed and every eye closed. Now, I'll be fair: the New Testament says almost nothing about how to eat the meal. But c'mon—I doubt it should be so mopey. There have been times during Communion when I've wondered, "Where's the body? Did I miss the casket?" Brothers and sisters, the Lord's Supper isn't a lamentation over a dead guy. He is alive! Communion is a celebration.

I'm all for tears of joy over what the Lord hath done to saveth my soul. Amen! Hallelujah! But too often we partake in the Lord's Supper as though we're at Jesus' wake. Communion isn't a time to feel condemnation; there is never time for that in Christ.[4] Jesus was condemned for us, and now we are more than conquerors because of him. The Lord's Table is a reminder that Jesus conquered our sin, Satan, and death. Communion is a festival of the new covenant. It's a gospelicious meal that is carbo-loaded with serious happiness.

> Communion is a festival of the new covenant. It's a gospelicious meal that is carbo-loaded with serious happiness.

King David got it: "Blessed is the one whose transgression is forgiven." Not gloomy is the man, nor somber, but happy! How happy is our meal? In general, Christians should smile more, but especially while eating the bread and drinking from the cup. Happy is the forgiven sinner, and his face will surely show it.

Let's be serious during Communion—serious about being forgiven. Seriously happy. At the Lord's Table, Jesus isn't looking for pity. He doesn't want it nor does he need it. He wants praise. Let's give it. Communion is celebration and preparation. Paul interprets the Lord's Supper as a sermon, a visual cue with two points: "For as often as you eat this bread and drink the cup, you proclaim the

---

4. "There is therefore now no condemnation for those who are in Christ Jesus" (Rom. 8:1).

Lord's death until he comes" (1 Cor. 11:26). The Table looks backward *and* forward. It's a proclamation of his death and the expectation of his return—"until he comes."

Comes for what?

To take his girl out to dinner.

Jesus is coming to get his bride and take her to the marriage supper of the Lamb. The Lord's Supper is far from a funeral meal; Communion is our rehearsal dinner for the great banquet to come.

Take and eat.

Enjoy.

Get ready—he's coming!

Celebrate the Lord Jesus. Eat the bread, drink the cup, be refreshed by his grace, and remember the Lord's death for you until he comes back to get you. This is worship.

> **Eat the bread, drink the cup, be refreshed by his grace.**

May you thank our Lord for the matchless and immeasurable kindness that has been extended to you through his cross. Whatever weighs you down, know this: God gives grace. Oh, he gives grace!

Remember this truth today: "I have been forgiven of all my sins, and there is now no condemnation for me—all because of Jesus." May it be said of you, "How happy is *that* Christian!"

The grace of the Lord Jesus be with you.

1 Corinthians 16:23

CHAPTER 10

Jesus Squashes
Our Idols

Little children, keep yourselves from idols.

1 JOHN 5:21

When was the last time you felt sorry for a cockroach? Grasshopper? Drawing a blank? Me too—until I read about this insane parasite that attacks beetles, grasshoppers, and the all-nasty cockroach. I won't bore you with the scientific name; we'll just call it the kamikaze worm.[1] I hate parasites just as much as the next guy, but this one is incredible.

The kamikaze worm invades its host and lives a peaceful, quiet life as it develops into mature wormhood. But once this parasite is ready to leave its host, it does so in a Shakespearean fashion. The kamikaze worm brainwashes its host to dive into the deep end of a nearby water source, causing the host's own death but the freedom of the worm. "Once in the water the mature hairworms—which are three to four times longer than their hosts when extended—emerge and swim away to find a mate, leaving their host dead or dying in the water."[2]

Wicked. This worm only comes to steal, kill, and destroy.

---

1. You really want the name, huh? Fine. *Spinochordodes tellinii*. Go ahead and Google your heart out.

2. Shaoni Bhattacharya, "Parasites Brainwash Grasshoppers into Death Dive," *New Scientist*, August 2005, http://www.newscientist.com/article/dn79 27#.Upu965Tf8Vk.

Our sins, idols, various temptations, and the satanic powers all have the same battle plan: get us to wreck ourselves. Satan knows we are free—"for freedom Christ has set us free"—and he knows that we are prone to forget the rest of Galatians 5:1: "Stand firm therefore, and do not submit again to a yoke of slavery." Jesus calls us to stand firm in our freedom, renouncing spiritual slavery to sin and idolatry. But we are prone to shift our gaze away from the cross toward our own golden calves. That is why the apostle John tells us to keep ourselves from idols (1 John 5:21).

> **Every temptation and sin involves idolatry; it is the most effective lure in Satan's tackle box.**

Every temptation and sin involves idolatry; it is the most effective lure in Satan's tackle box. Our pimply foe has multiple PhDs in deception, and he is *the* expert on luring people into idol worship.

Satan uses more than mossy, weather-beaten statues; he also moves people to worship creation—the sun, moon, stars, etc. But he doesn't stop there, especially in dealing with Christians in the twenty-first century. He knows you and I won't worship a boring statue, but we might worship something similar if it brings us entertainment like sports, movies, and sitcoms. Satan and his servants know we won't dare worship a god from another religion—unless they help us create our own god and our own religion: a "faith" that makes us feel happy with no concern for being holy, or a religious rigmarole to earn God's love, or a spirituality without Jesus at the center. Something we can handle.

This is serious business, which is why John implores the children of God to stand guard against idolatry. Idolatry is taking anything other than the true God of the Bible and making it ultimate in your life. It can be anything—jobs, electronics, dreams, kids, body image, reputation, and worst of all, a cobbled-together religious Franken-god. We are prone to chase long-lasting satisfaction in Juicy Fruit pleasures, here and then gone. The demons calculate their plan to get us all twisted up. As the senior demon Screwtape instructed his nephew, "An ever increasing craving for an ever diminishing pleasure is the formula."[3] We need to stand guard and renew our minds in the glories of Christ (Rom. 12:1–2).

The apostle John exhorted a small group of first-century Christians to keep themselves from idols. The Greek word translated "keep" means to guard or protect. God wants Christians to fortify their lives against idols. We can't be passive in the war against idolatry; passivity grants idols a pass. God wants a moat filled with alligators to surround your heart. He wants bulletproof glass on all of your windows. He wants security cameras, laser sensors, pressure monitors, and thumb scanners all over the home of your heart. Your heart should resemble a fortress where only the true and living God is allowed entrance.

But before you go out and make more rules for yourself, know this: the best way to fend off the worship of idols is to be consumed with worshiping the living God of the gospel. Grace is preloaded with power against idolatry. Christian growth is not like a combo-lock. We don't change by dialing in the right amount of Bible reading, prayer, Scripture memory, service, and community, and then *click*. By all means, do the spiritual disciplines, but know that the spiritual disciplines aren't what change us. We are transformed, and idols are shattered, by what the disciplines are meant to show us: the glory of Jesus. The disciplines are vehicles of faith, means of grace to get us on the path of the Spirit so we can behold, see, and feel the wonder of Christ.

> **The best way to fend off the worship of idols is to be consumed with worshiping the living God of the gospel.**

According to Paul, gazing upon the Lord's glory changes us:

3. C.S. Lewis, *The Screwtape Letters* (New York: HarperCollins, 2001), 44.

"We all, with unveiled face, beholding the glory of the Lord, are being transformed into the same image from one degree of glory to another" (2 Cor. 3:18). Growth is fueled when we are filled with the glory of Jesus. Fixating on Jesus is our duty. The seventeenth-century theologian John Owen wrote, "For there is no more certain gospel truth than this, that believers ought continually to contemplate on Christ by the actings of faith in their thoughts and affections, and that thereby they are changed and transformed into his image."[4]

We need to look deeply at the gospel, into the person and work of Jesus. Let your eyes linger on that bloodstained cross. Move your heart next to his heart, pierced for you. Keep hearing his proclamation, "It is finished!" until revival begins and temptations are weakened. Gospel-centered growth is energized by a Christ-centered fixation. The glory of Christ is the hypersonic fuel of real Christian growth.

Now, I have a confession, and I hope revealing my spiritual stupidity serves you. For years—years!—I read the Bible, memorized verses, *tried* to pray like a monk (I never got close), and went to church three times a week.

And I forgot all about Jesus.

Guess how much I grew, changed, and matured? Zero. Zilch. *Nada*.

But when the high-octane power of gospel wakefulness[5] captured my heart—everything changed. Personal revival happened. Once I heard that the gospel was also for my sanctification, all of a sudden Jesus became exciting. I *wanted* to follow him. I *really wanted* to be conformed to his image. And for the first time, I knew that in order to look like him, I would need him daily. Go figure.

The truth is so simple, yet we've all overlooked it: We can't be like Jesus without Jesus. Oh, how we try. But gospel-centered living

---

4. John Owen, *The Works of John Owen*, ed. William H. Goold, vol. 7 (Edinburgh: T&T Clark, n.d.), 346.

5. You should buy *Gospel Wakefulness* by Jared C. Wilson—right now. Or finish this chapter and then go. Whichever works best for you.

throws in the towel on self-help, *sola bootstrapa*, and all of our "I'm okay"-ness. And it pleads for the power of Jesus in our lives. Beholding the glories of the gospel will change your Christianity for the better, to what it's meant to be. If Jesus doesn't rock you, keep looking. Ask him to blow you away. I bet he'll answer that prayer. And while you're at it, honestly ask yourself if something else is taking your breath away—because if Jesus doesn't, something else is. Find it. Confess it. Repent of it.

And behold Jesus anew.

Once you've beheld, you'll never be the same. Sin becomes less appetizing. The things of earth begin to grow strangely dim, and the things of God take on a Holy Ghost gravitational

> **The truth is so simple, yet we've all overlooked it: We can't be like Jesus without Jesus.**

pull. The Bible moves from being a boring old book to kindling for worship. Singing ceases to be an awkward ordeal and becomes an act of abounding exultation over your God and King. Serving is no longer an obligation but an opportunity to love others.

Jesus changes the way we are changed. The gospel really does change everything. Trying to change without treasuring Christ is no way to live. You need grace, not grit; not mere rules, but the Ruler and his gentle commands. You need Jesus.

Use what he has already given you. Swing the sword of the Spirit, the Word of God, to attack, disarm, or slay any

> **Jesus changes the way we are changed.**

idols that try to take you hostage. Call in reinforcements. You need friends, a real community of Christians to help you fight. Radio in an army of believers to help you wage the war and fight the good fight. They can watch your back, and they will pull you back when you try to open the front door of your heart to the ancient Snake Oil Salesman. Friends can help you do a clean sweep of the premises to make sure all the rooms are clear.

Keep yourself from idols. Fortify yourself against idols. Kill any idols that are loitering on the property of your heart.

May you worship the Father, the Son, and the Spirit only, because in them alone is where life is found.

Only take care, and keep your soul diligently, lest you forget the things that your eyes have seen, and lest they depart from your heart all the days of your life.

DEUTERONOMY 4:9

CHAPTER 11

Whether You Eat or Drink

*So, whether you eat or drink, or whatever
you do, do all to the glory of God.*

1 CORINTHIANS 10:31

When I say, "It's all about Jesus," it's because Jesus is the Lord. He holds every right to say, "Hey, that doesn't honor me. I love you. But that needs to change." Jesus approves of us sinners because we are in him, but he doesn't approve of our sin. Lives that are all about Jesus will be lives that fight against things that aren't about Jesus. We make it our aim to please him (2 Cor. 5:9). We worship Jesus in *all* of life.

Jesus is Lord over everything, not some things. Jesus is to be honored in our bedrooms: "Let marriage be held in honor among all, and let the marriage bed be undefiled, for God will judge the sexually immoral and adulterous" (Heb. 13:4). He is Lord over our bank accounts: "Keep your life free from love of money, and be content with what you have, for he has said, 'I will never leave you nor forsake you'" (Heb. 13:5). Jesus goes against the grain of our rotten hearts, our blind spots, and our bizarre church cultures.

> **Jesus is Lord over everything, not some things.**

I think it's funny when someone says, "I don't mean to offend you" or "I don't mean to hit a nerve," and then they proceed to offend and damage our nerves. The gospel is more honest, because Jesus intends to cut to the point: "The word of God is living and active, sharper than any two-edged sword, piercing to the division of soul and of spirit, of joints and of marrow, and discerning the thoughts and intentions of the heart. And no creature is hidden from his sight, but all are naked and exposed to the eyes of him to whom we must give account" (Heb. 4:12–13). We live our lives in his sight, and bearing this in mind, grace-addicted people don't take the reality of grace as a free pass. Rather, it is seen as freedom to pursue what pleases Jesus and is for our good. The gospel creates holy people. We are being washed in the water of the Word by the Son of God (Eph. 5:26).

That applies to all aspects of life, including a rotund area that we readily overlook: food. Maybe you don't struggle with overeating, but there are many who do. So it bears pointing out that Jesus reigns over the pantry as well as the prayer closet.

The gospel declares that Jesus is Lord, meaning he's also to be Lord of what we put in our mouths—the "whatever" in "whatever [we] eat or drink" (1 Cor. 10:31). Listen to this odd (but true) riff from C.S. Lewis: "You can get a large audience together for a strip-tease act—that is, to watch a girl undress on the stage. Now suppose you came to a country where you could fill a theatre by simply bringing a covered plate on to the stage and then slowly lifting the cover so as to let every one see, just before the lights went out, that it contained a mutton chop or a bit of bacon, would you not think that in that country something had gone wrong with the appetite for food?"[1]

Picture a church's fellowship hall packed with high-cholesterol congregants fawning over an ice-cream-eating contest, all while starting their diets on Monday. These people are unhealthy, they know it, and they are hopping on the elliptical wagon next week. But as for today . . .

Would you think something had gone wrong with these believers' appetite for food?

---

1. C.S. Lewis, *Mere Christianity* (New York: HarperCollins, 2001), 96.

Or imagine a married man whose Internet devices put him a mere click away from iniquity. With no blockers, no accountability, and no one to ask this man about his lust, he indulges often. Would you say something had gone wrong with his appetite for women?

Where is the Lord Jesus in these imbalances? He's knocking, ready to make his presence known. "Behold, I stand at the door and knock. If anyone hears my voice and opens the door, I will come in to him and eat with him, and he with me" (Rev. 3:20).

We shudder at the thought of high school kids flipping through centerfolds in the toolshed behind the church's family life center, and we should. But why don't we have the same reaction to the father of four who is 150 pounds overweight and getting his third helping of blackberry cobbler and ice cream right before our eyes? We show concern for the anorexic and bulimic but ignore the obese. This should not be. Do we have some repenting to do?

When we see Jesus as the Lord, we show a humble and zealous concern for every sin in our hearts. The gospel has a way of leveling out our conception of crimes against the Holy One. The uneven scales get smashed (Prov. 20:23). Only Jesus can give us the right eyes and taste buds when it comes to physical health—and only Jesus can give us the right spiritual taste buds when it comes to our pursuit of holiness. Moralism won't cut it.

> Only Jesus can give us the right spiritual taste buds when it comes to our pursuit of holiness. Moralism won't cut it.

"Nothing tastes as good as being skinny feels." That's a load of mumbo-jumbo: I've had cheesecake before. *Everything* tastes better than being skinny feels, because being skinny isn't the chief end. Glorifying God is. Nothing tastes as good as glorying the Lord feels (1 Cor. 10:31).

Telling a man to "bounce his eyes" instead of drooling over a woman is ultimately not helpful. The problem is in the heart, not the eyes. The glutton's issue isn't his gut—it's his heart, "for out of the heart come evil thoughts, murder, adultery, sexual immorality, theft, false witness, slander" (Matt. 15:19). The reason to pursue healthy living isn't solely for being skinny, looking better during the summer, and so on; the reason is that our bodies, our hearts, and everything else about us are not our own. They belong to Jesus.

Another way to say it would be this: Pursue healthiness because of holiness. The gospel of the kingdom reminds me that my life is not mine—it's his, and it's to be used for the name, glory, and mission of Christ.

Worship makes war on our sins. As many have said, "We worship our way into sin, and we have to worship our way out of it." But one of our biggest hurdles to crucifying a sin is our failure to see it as sinful. If we aren't watchful, we can become skilled at the self-deception required to excuse sin.

We must get to where we can say, "My eating habits/spending habits/attitudes are sinful. They're out of control. My weight/stewardship/Internet usage is sinful. I'm sinning against my spouse/kids/community, and my Lord. Forgive me, Lord. Empower me to honor you—to be a faithful steward of this body/money you've given me, for your glory and my good."

Until we walk in the light and are honest with ourselves and others, we will continue to get nowhere. Because sin will never take it easy on us. It works overtime looking for ways to seep further into our thinking. That is why the apostle Paul admonishes us, in Romans 8:13, to "put to death the deeds of the body." Commenting on that verse, John Owen wrote, "Make it your daily work; be always at it whilst you live; cease not a day from this work; be killing sin or it will be killing you."[2]

Do not wait until Monday to repent and pursue godliness. Today

---

2. John Owen, *The Works of John Owen*, ed. William H. Goold, vol. 6 (Edinburgh: T&T Clark, n.d.), 9.

belongs to the Lord; you may not have Monday (James 4:14). And putting off the pursuit of holiness will only perpetuate your current unreality, ensuring that your life remains overgrown and a mess. As Solomon writes,

> I passed by the field of a sluggard,
>> by the vineyard of a man lacking sense,
> and behold, it was all overgrown with thorns;
>> the ground was covered with nettles,
>> and its stone wall was broken down.
> Then I saw and considered it;
>> I looked and received instruction.
> A little sleep, a little slumber,
>> a little folding of the hands to rest,
> and poverty will come upon you like a robber,
>> and want like an armed man.
>> (Prov. 24:30–34)

To be sluggardly is to self-destruct. Whatever your struggle, there is hope. There's always hope. The same gospel of grace that changed the disciples and that changes drug addicts, adulterers, porn stars, gangsters, and gluttons as well as venture capitalists, plumbers, and homeschool moms is alive and well, and its power is Jesus. If you are entangled in a sin, then do what the book of Hebrews says and look to him (Heb. 12:1–4). Caloric counters, pornography-blocking software, and accountability groups are all great tools, but they cannot change the soul. If you want real help, look to Jesus of Nazareth: "Consider yourselves dead to sin and alive to God in Christ Jesus" (Rom. 6:11). We all have to do this. Jesus is our hope—and our Lord.

Whatever your struggle, there is hope. There's always hope.

The gospel of the kingdom goes into every nook and cranny of life; the reign of Christ extends to all its edges—food, sex, entertainment, Netflix, hobbies, books, *everything*.

The power of Christ is for our everyday moments, the "whatever" we eat, drink, or do. And when we fail, sin, and fall short—when we overdo our calories, watch what isn't for our eyes, buy what our wallet can't handle, or in different ways trade our joy in Christ for a bowl of red stew (Gen. 25:29–34)—then there is "no condemnation for those who are in Christ Jesus" (Rom. 8:1). That's good news, a supersized reason to worship.

May you eat, drink, and be merry—and worship your Lord.

---

*So put away all malice and all deceit and hypocrisy
and envy and all slander. Like newborn infants, long
for the pure spiritual milk, that by it you may grow up
into salvation—if indeed you have tasted that the
Lord is good.*

1 Peter 2:1–3

CHAPTER 12

The Forever-Fullness of Jesus

*You make known to me the path of life; in
your presence there is fullness of joy; at your
right hand are pleasures forevermore.*

PSALM 16:11

Forevermore? Sounds like a fairy tale doesn't it? "At your right hand
I'll live happily ever after."

Well, forever-fullness is no myth. Gladness of this magnitude
is too good to be false, and the Bible
doesn't kid around about it. King David
is onto something. He tells us where
fullness of joy and pleasures forevermore
can be found. When it comes to the real
estate of joy, it's all about location, location, location. Only in God's presence
is there thoroughness, a richness, to joy. David isn't selling us on
never-ending droplets of joy. This is a *gushing* joy. Jumbo-sized joy
is in God's presence.

> When it comes to the
> real estate of joy, it's
> all about location,
> location, location.

The only way to have this joy is through the Way, the Truth, and
the Life.[1] If this joy is in God's presence, the gospel is what takes us
there—there is no other way to God. Jesus walked the Calvary road

---

1. "Jesus said to him, 'I am the way, and the truth, and the life. No one comes
to the Father except through me'" (John 14:6).

and stepped out of the tomb to bring us to God.[2] The gospel gives us access to the only joy in existence that can provide the hearty fulfillment our souls seek.

This everlasting gladness is found at a location even more specific than God's presence: "At your *right hand* are pleasures forevermore" (italics mine). What is at God's right hand? Or better yet, *who* is at God's right hand? "Jesus, the founder and perfecter of our faith, who for the joy that was set before him endured the cross, despising the shame, and is *seated at the right hand of the throne of God*" (Heb. 12:2, italics mine).

Jesus is not only the access to the wellspring of joy—he *is* the joy. He is the way and the reward. God the Son is the great pleasure of God's people. The phrase "gospel-centered joy" hardly needs explaining. Jesus is the source and subject of our joy.

Who has done more for us than Jesus? Who's ever come close? No one loves like Jesus. No one and nothing delivers on their promises like Jesus. The good news of forgiveness from all of our crimes, being made a child of God and a co-heir with Christ, does the heart good. Forever. Jesus has wounded the Dragon, and he is coming back to get his girl, his beautiful church.

The Bible is the tale of tales. A Jesus-exalting view of the Bible means that you refuse to view the Bible (and the Christian experience) as mere regulations and sanctions for life on earth. The Bible is way more than that. Children's book author Sally Lloyd-Jones says it best:

> No, the Bible isn't a book of rules, or a book of heroes.
> The Bible is most of all a Story. It's an adventure story
> about a young Hero who comes from a far country to

---

2. "For Christ also suffered once for sins, the righteous for the unrighteous, that he might bring us to God, being put to death in the flesh but made alive in the spirit" (1 Peter 3:18).

win back his lost treasure. It's a love story about a brave Prince who leaves his palace, his throne—everything— to rescue the ones he loves. It's like the most wonderful of fairy tales that has come true in real life!

You see, the best thing about this Story is—it's true.

There are lots of stories in the Bible, but all the stories are telling one Big Story. The Story of how God loves his children and comes to rescue them.

It takes the whole Bible to tell this Story. And at the center of the Story, there is a baby. Every story in the Bible whispers his name. He is like the missing piece in the puzzle—the piece that makes all the other pieces fit together, and suddenly you can see a beautiful picture.[3]

What beautiful picture? A crucified, risen, sin-pardoning hero— your hero. Your Savior. Your Jesus, and he killed the big bad wolf. Your sin is finished. Do you believe it? As in all good tales, the enemy is vanquished. It's time to believe it—that's part of the "happily ever after."

> As in all good tales, the enemy is vanquished. It's time to believe it – that's part of the "happily ever after."

How would you describe your relationship with sin? For the Christian, only one word in the Bible fits: deceased. God's Word doesn't say that we are simply weakened, cold, hardened, or numb to sin; it declares that we are *dead* to sin and *alive* to God because of Jesus. "So you also must consider yourselves dead to sin and alive to God in Christ Jesus" (Rom. 6:11). If you're like me, you probably don't always feel this way toward sin, but the gospel brings great news. You are

---

3. Sally Lloyd-Jones, *The Jesus StoryBook Bible* (Grand Rapids: Zondervan, 2007), 17.

no longer under the power, control, and kingdom of Satan and his toxic meal-deals.

If you are in Christ, look at how the Bible describes your relationship with sin. I heard these from the great Scottish theologian Sinclair Ferguson, in a seminary class, and I pass them on to you:

- Sin is no longer your *king*: "Let not sin therefore *reign*" (Rom. 6:12).
- Sin is not your *commander*: "Do not present your members to sin as *instruments* [weapons]" (v. 13).
- Sin is done being your *dictator*: "For sin will have no *dominion* over you" (v. 14).
- Sin is no longer your *master*: "You were *slaves* of sin" (v. 20).
- Sin is no longer your *employer*: "The *wages* of sin is death" (v. 23).

Sin controlled you, but no more. You are free. Jesus smashed sin's scepter, and now he reigns *forever*. The Lion of Judah roars against all other predators.

> Go back to the gospel – again. Not for conversion, but for comfort.

But maybe you don't feel like you are dead to sin. There is hope. If you are a Christian and your life still sleeps in the pigpen—it is time to confess, repent,[4] and walk in the freedom that Jesus has already purchased for you.[5] Go back to the gospel—again. Not for conversion, but for comfort. The gospel—Jesus' death and resurrection—is a one-time event, but we believe it more

---

4. "If we say we have no sin, we deceive ourselves, and the truth is not in us. If we confess our sins, he is faithful and just to forgive us our sins and to cleanse us from all unrighteousness" (1 John 1:8–10).

5. "For freedom Christ has set us free; stand firm therefore, and do not submit again to a yoke of slavery" (Gal. 5:1).

than once—we believe it and re-believe it every day. God's gospel declares that you are free. You are safe in Christ, and he is ready to help you. Go to God. Cherish the foreverness of Jesus' work for you, walk in grace, and life change is on the way. In fact, it has already touched down.

Paul's instruction from Romans 6:11 is clear: "You also must consider yourselves dead to sin and alive to God in Christ Jesus." Believe it. Don't close this book till you do. Your being dead to sin is as true and real as Jesus being alive. Christian, you *must* consider your ties with sin to be forever severed by the blood of Jesus. This is what it means to believe the gospel again—believing the glorious gifts of the gospel.

We will still sin, and Jesus will continue to own us. Sin is no match for Jesus. He's already shown what he can do. Jesus is bigger, stronger, faster, and greater than all our sin: "For you have died, and your life is hidden with Christ in God" (Col. 3:3). Do you believe that you are dead to sin? Do you believe that you are alive? What sin do you think you'll never have victory over? Today that lie ends; the crimson flood swallows it up—your joy is found in gospel truth. Jesus is the great curse-lifter promised in the garden of Eden (Gen. 3:15), the great gloom-cleanser of the land, the heavenly and human harbinger of joy.

> Gospel joy doesn't have an expiration date because Jesus undid his personal expiry in the resurrection.

Gospel joy doesn't have an expiration date because Jesus undid his personal expiry in the resurrection. Our joy keeps rising because we too won't expire; we have a new identity in him and with him. We'll live forever in his fullness and be forever filled with his glory. He is the joy of joys, the King of joy, and he'll make us happy ever after.

May you experience the exhilarating joy that is God. Look to Jesus, where you'll find pleasures forevermore.

Satisfy us in the morning with your steadfast love,
that we may rejoice and be glad all our days.

PSALM 90:14

PART THREE

What Is
Gospel Identity?

Gospel identity is discovering the Christian's meaning, purpose, acceptance with God, and position in the universe based on our union with Christ.

Gospel identity is first, foremost, and always that we are "in Christ."

CHAPTER 13

Gospel Identity

He is not ashamed to call them brothers.

HEBREWS 2:11

Have you ever thought about the meaning of your name? My wife's name, Natalie, means "child of Christmas." (Cute, but she was born in March.[1])

Names in the Bible are often pregnant with significance. Naming a child ranged from a parent's reaction at birth (Isaac means "laughter") to religious affiliation (Adonijah means "the Lord is sovereign"). In the ancient Near East, your name defined you.

But what about when someone's name is changed? God has a thing for changing names.

- "'No longer shall your name be called Abram, but your name shall be Abraham'" (Gen. 17:5).
- "He said, 'Your name shall no longer be called Jacob, but Israel'" (Gen. 32:28).
- "God said to Abraham, 'As for Sarai your wife, you shall not call her name Sarai, but Sarah shall be her name'" (Gen. 17:15).
- "Jesus looked at him and said, 'You are Simon the son of John. You shall be called Cephas' (which means Peter)" (John 1:42).

---

1. I love you, babe.

What's all the fuss about a new name? It's mega-crucial. A new name from God means you've been redefined. God grants a new identity, a new life, a new outlook. For instance, every time Abram heard his new name—Abraham, "the father of a multitude"—he would hear and remember God's promise to him that he would be the father of many. Abraham was given a new identity by God, wrapped in a promise from God that would be kept by God.

> A new name from God means you've been redefined. God grants a new identity, a new life, a new outlook.

Christian, you have a new name. "So you are no longer a slave, but a *son*, and if a son, then an *heir* through God" (Gal. 4:7). "See what kind of love the Father has given to us, that we should be called *children of God*; and so we are" (1 John 3:1). "No longer do I call you servants, for the servant does not know what his master is doing; but I have called you *friends*" (John 15:15; all italics mine).

Do you know who you are? What defines your life—or rather, *who* defines your life?

All of your hurts, hang-ups, disappointments, and struggles do not make up who you are. Only Jesus does. If you are in Christ, you are no longer defined by your sins, whether past, present, or future. Jesus gives you a new identity. Yet far too often we mislabel ourselves and others.

Have you ever called yourself a liar? Have you ever labeled another Christian an adulterer? What about a drunkard—or in today's language, an alcoholic? Or a homosexual? Thinking this way does more damage than we realize. I know because I myself have suffered at the hand of the same cruel label master. Maybe you can hear yourself saying,

- "I'm so arrogant."
- "I'm a proud jerk."

- "I'm such a fool."
- "You are ____."

'That line of thinking is anti-gospel. It defines us by our sins rather than the conquering power of Christ on the cross. By looking inward instead of upward, fixating on our sins instead of Jesus, we are subtly drawn away from the power of Christ. The accusations of Satan, ourselves, and others—"You are a (pick the sin of your choice)"— seek to identify us with sin instead of with Jesus, who became our sin for us. But the sin identity is a false identity. The truth is, we are no longer our sin. Rather, we are the pure righteousness of Christ.[2] Grace means that we are not defined by our sins but by Jesus, who became our sin in his death and then rose from the dead in sinless victory.

> **The truth is, we are no longer our sin. Rather, we are the pure righteousness of Christ.**

This does not belittle our indwelling sins; rather, it puts them in the right perspective. We must wage war against our sin, but we must also think of sin rightly. We are what Martin Luther called *simul iustus et peccator* (at the same time righteous and a sinner). We are saints *and* sinners. We are no longer *just* sinners. We are sinners saved by grace.

The apostle Paul wanted the Corinthian Christians to grasp this very thing. In 1 Corinthians 6, he rattles off a list of sins and then drops a four-letter, megaton word on them: "And such *were* some of you."

"Were" is the game changer. The Corinthians *were* sexually immoral, idolaters, drunkards, thieves, etc. Those sins used to define them—but not anymore, because another "were" had crashed into

---

2. "For our sake [God] made [Jesus] to be sin who knew no sin, so that in him we might become the righteousness of God" (2 Cor. 5:21).

their lives. The Corinthian Christians *were* washed, sanctified, and justified in the name of the Lord Jesus by the Holy Spirit. And if you are in Jesus, the same is true of you. As the blood of Jesus flowed down the cross, it washed away all of our sin stains. Now we are new people in Jesus.

This isn't mere church talk. The glories of the gospel impact the way we carry ourselves. The gospel keeps us from dragging our knuckles, and it lifts our chins up. For example, if you are in Christ and drunkenness entangles you, you nevertheless are not a drunkard. You are a child of God who has been redeemed by the blood of Jesus and has committed a sin. That sin doesn't define you. Jesus does. And he wants you to confess, repent, and walk in a forgiveness you can feel.

Gospel-centeredness means we go back to the cross and find ourselves there, not in our sin. When we sin, we go back to Calvary and believe that we are forgiven, cleansed, saved, and redeemed from all that haunts us. Jesus changes the way we think about our sin, ourselves, and our brothers and sisters who are also in Christ. That man isn't an adulterer; he is a Christian who committed adultery, and the blood of Jesus washes him clean. That woman in your small group isn't an arrogant person; she is a Christian who wrestles with pride. The world wants us to define ourselves and each other by our sins, but God does not (Rom. 8:1).

> **The world wants us to define ourselves and each other by our sins, but God does not.**

"Hi, I'm Tom, and I'm an alcoholic." That's anti-gospel. "Hi, I'm John and I have been saved by Jesus, cleansed by his blood, freed, redeemed, and justified by his name. I struggle with drunkenness. It's a sin, and I hate it. But I know Jesus is bigger. I believe he has forgiven me, and he loves me just the same. And I have faith that he will help me." That's gospel living. This kind of thinking leads to changed lives. It woos us toward the kindness of God, biblical repentance, and the power to change.

Grace-addicted living is wholly defined not by our sins but by our union with Jesus. We are now known as those who are "in Christ." We are the crucified-with-him, the forgiven, the born-again, the redeemed. The gospel calls us to lay down our man-made definitions and cling to what God says of us. Our self-introspection only leaves us with a heap of condemnation. But when we go to Jesus, we find the hope of the gospel. We find our new life.

Do you believe this about yourself?

Do you believe this about others?

Do you define yourself by your sins or by your Savior?

Do you think of others as being more "in sin" or "in Christ"?

Whatever old names you had, forget them. I mean, all of 'em. Addict, adulterer, liar, cheater, drunkard, pervert, victim, moralist, bully, Pharisee, depressed, glutton, pill-popper—shun those names. They might be sins you struggle with, but they aren't your calling card. They're who you *were*, not who you are now in light of the gospel. Jesus took the old you into the ground, and a new you came up with him.

May you remember your new names today. Behold your Savior and what he says about you. Rejoice and live again.

Do not be deceived: neither the sexually immoral, nor idolaters, nor adulterers, nor men who practice homosexuality, nor thieves, nor the greedy, nor drunkards, nor revilers, nor swindlers will inherit the kingdom of God. And such were some of you. But you were washed, you were sanctified, you were justified in the name of the Lord Jesus Christ and by the Spirit of our God.

1 CORINTHIANS 6:9–11

CHAPTER 14

You Are Greatly Loved

*"At the beginning of your pleas for mercy a
word went out, [Daniel,] and I have come to
tell it to you, for you are greatly loved."*

Daniel 9:23

On Valentine's Day, John Johnston always gave his wife, Sue, a lovely arrangement of flowers. Very thoughtful, right? Except that in John's case, "thoughtful" only begins to describe his bouquets. His wife says it best:

> My Sweet husband, John, and I were married for 46 years. Each Valentine's Day, he'd send me the most beautiful flowers containing a note with five simple words: "My love for you grows." Four children, 46 bouquets and a lifetime of love were his legacy to me when he passed away two years ago.
>
> On my first Valentine's Day alone, 10 months after I lost him, I was shocked to receive a gorgeous bouquet addressed to me . . . from John. Angry and heartbroken, I called the florist to say there had been a mistake. The florist replied, "No, ma'am, it's not a mistake. Before he passed away, your husband pre-paid for many years and asked us to guarantee that you'd continue getting bouquets every Valentine's Day." With my heart in my throat, I hung up the

phone and read the attached card. It said, "My love for you is eternal."[1]

That's more than thoughtful—it's incredible. John's forward thinking and love for his bride is an amazing story. Every Valentine's Day, and for as long as the flowers in each arrangement last, Sue is reminded of her husband's great love for her.

Today, the gospel stands as God's bouquet of love for you. It doesn't come wrapped in plastic but in flesh. There are no red roses, just red blood. There is no vase, only a cross. The man on that cross is our gift. And his words to us, his beloved, are, "My love for you is eternal."

> **The gospel stands as God's bouquet of love for you.**

Today God wants to make his love abundantly clear to you. Christian, you are greatly loved. Imagine God showing up one day and saying that to you: "You are greatly loved." Not just once but three times. That is what happened to the prophet Daniel:

- "You are greatly loved" (Dan. 9.23).
- "And he said to me, 'O Daniel, man greatly loved . . .'" (Dan. 10:11).
- "And he said, 'O man greatly loved . . .'" (Dan. 10:19).

You think Daniel got the message? God wanted to make his love for Daniel—his *great* love—abundantly clear.

God feels the same way about you. He wants to show you his immeasurable love. It's a massive love. Grand. Heavy. And it's more than words alone. Jesus not only told you he loves you—he also

---

1. Hayley Hudson, "Valentine's Gesture from Dead Husband to Wife Will Make You Melt," *Huffington Post*, February 10, 2013, http://www.huffingtonpost .com/2013/02/10/dead-husband-valentine_n_2654726.html.

showed you by living out his words: "Greater love has no one than this, that someone lay down his life for his friends" (John 15:13).

Daniel walked away confident of God's great love for him because God made it clear to him. God has done so for you as well. Anytime you doubt the great love of God for you, there is one place to always look—Calvary. The cross is the pulpit sermon of God's matchless love for you. You don't have to do anything to earn God's love. He loved you before you were born. He loves you right now. Believe it.[2] What Paul wrote to the believers at Ephesus, he would say to you as well:

> But God, being rich in mercy, because of the great love with which he loved us, even when we were dead in our trespasses, made us alive together with Christ—by grace you have been saved—and raised us up with him and seated us with him in the heavenly places in Christ Jesus, so that in the coming ages he might show the immeasurable riches of his grace in kindness toward us in Christ Jesus. (Eph. 2:4–7)

Galatians 2:20 is unquestionably the Bible verse that has changed my life the most. It flips my world right-side up. Paul's words are a spiritual epi-pen for floundering hearts.[3] He writes, "I have been crucified with Christ. It is no longer I who live, but Christ who lives in me. And the life I now live in the flesh I live by faith in the Son of God, who loved me and gave himself for me." The glories of this verse are worth marinating in again and again. No Christian has ever felt too loved, too blessed, too forgiven—the

---

2. "We have come to know and to believe the love that God has for us" (1 John 4:16).

3. An epi-pen is a medical device used to quickly inject a dose of epinephrine to save a person going into shock. I like to think of the gospel as an epi-pen to a Christian's sluggish heart.

goodness of God keeps piling on us. In the words of the sixteenth century theologian Samuel Rutherford, "Acquaint yourself with Christ's love, and ye shall not miss to find new goldmines and treasures in Christ."[4]

Christian, your identity is wholly found in Christ. He alone defines who you are. Nothing else does. No accomplishments, titles, wins, failures, or sins define you. It's all Jesus. Your old self died and Jesus is alive in you. In a sense, you don't even exist anymore. The old you is off the grid; he's gone dark, never to surface again. When Jesus hung on that blood-soaked tree, you were there too as a dying participant. And when he rose from the grave, you were right behind him. Christianity is a religion of coattails; we cling to a Galilean carpenter's coat all the way to heaven.

We no longer grind our gears in Christian growth and maturity, as though it were all up to us. The gospel illuminates the path for all Christian growth, and that path is the God-man, Christ Jesus. We grow because it is God who works in us.[5] How loving! God supplies what God demands. Gospel-centeredness checks us out from the school of sweat-equity sanctification and into the school of grace.

> Gospel-centeredness checks us out from the school of sweat-equity sanctification and into the school of grace.

We are invited to go to the One who is at work in us, the One who is alive in you and me right now.

"He loved *me* and gave himself *for me*"—there are no more powerful words for the soul. They are what activated my obsession with

---

4. Samuel Rutherford, *The Loveliness of Christ* (Edinburgh: The Banner of Truth Trust, 2008), 66.
5. "Therefore, my beloved, as you have always obeyed, so now, not only as in my presence but much more in my absence, work out your own salvation with fear and trembling, for it is God who works in you, both to will and to work for his good pleasure" (Phil. 2:12–13).

Jesus, and once you are dialed in to their truth, your own world will never be the same. When your heart is stalling, reach for this gospel epi-pen: *Jesus loves me, this I know, and the Bible really does tell me so.* Let that be your mantra.

Gospel worship is a response to God's love—the good news of God the Son dying and rising for sinners. Gospel-powered worship melts the icy worship that results from legalism. True worship springs out of two blazing reactors of love: God's love for us and *then* our love for him. The former fuels the latter. Our love for him can only be sparked and sustained by his love for us.

The apostles Paul and John help tie this together. Paul: "God shows his love for us in that while we were still sinners, Christ died for us" (Rom. 5:8). And John: "In this the love of God was made manifest among us, that God sent his only Son into the world, so that we might live through him. In this is love, not that we have loved God but that he loved us and sent his Son to be the propitiation for our sins" (1 John 4:9–10). And, "We love because he first loved us" (1 John 4:19).

God's love not only sets our own love for him ablaze, but it also sustains that love. We keep loving God because he keeps loving us. We wouldn't even know what love is if it weren't for God. The unmerited, matchless, immeasurable, unparalleled love of God for you is why you love him.

Are you blown away that Jesus loves you? That he gave himself for you? Do you struggle to believe that Jesus loves you? The gospel tells you every morning, "Oh, Christian! You are greatly loved."

May you know today that you are greatly loved by the Great One in his greatest act of love.

The LORD your God will circumcise your heart and the heart of your offspring, so that you will love the LORD your God with all your heart and with all your soul, that you may live.

DEUTERONOMY 30:6

CHAPTER 15

God Comforts You, His Child

He will wipe away every tear from their eyes, and death shall be no more, neither shall there be mourning, nor crying, nor pain anymore, for the former things have passed away.

REVELATION 21:4

Larry Asher gave me guitar lessons back in high school. I was your typical youth grouper. I played guitar, I sang, and I wore a pre-torn hat from American Eagle. Larry taught me how to play the songs we were singing at church. He also taught me how to play Hendrix, Nirvana, and Santana. I looked forward to lessons with Larry. He taught me how to use my axe.

And then a few years later, Larry died. He had been changing a flat tire on a towering off-ramp that sprawled across Interstate 45, one of the busiest freeways in Houston. Eyewitnesses said his spare fell off the overpass, and when Larry tried to grab it, he lost his balance and fell to instant death right in the middle of morning traffic on I-45.

When my mom sent me the news of Larry's passing, I was sitting on the couch, and I said to my wife, Natalie, "Praise the Lord that Larry was a Christian." Then I stopped myself. "No, no. Praise the Lord that Larry *is* a Christian."

Larry is still a Christian. Right now, Larry Asher *is*. And he *is* because Jesus *is*. There is no past tense with Larry or with anyone who is in Christ. There is only the present and future, and they are glorious. The gospel redeems us from our past, and it lodges us in a corrosion-proof reality. Sure, our bodies will erode, but we will not. As children of the living God, we will live forever with him.

The beauty of being a child of God is that our Father comforts us in all things. Our world and our lives are riddled with pain; we are plagued by hurts, hang-ups, tears, death, and mourning. But the gospel gives us hope. Grace fits every occasion, Christ cares about everything in our lives, and gospel promises are engineered to lift up our souls. So if you aren't weighed down today, take the Bible's truths and store them up, for the storm is sure to come. And there will be fellow believers who also need gospel wisdom from you in the future.

> Grace fits every occasion, Christ cares about everything in our lives, and gospel promises are engineered to lift up our souls.

God's promises about eternity are meant to help you get through yesterday, today, and tomorrow. Events that have passed may have left a hurt that remains. But God is no stranger to what you go through. God the Son came to earth and lived among us, and he experienced what you do. Jesus cried over the death of his friend Lazarus. Those closest to him deserted him. Jesus felt the greatest pain imaginable. He knows what it's like, and he has a tender heart for hurting people.[1]

When God brings you into eternity, he will wipe away all of your past pains and usher you into a life where you will never feel the fallen-ness of earth again. God is going to do something incredible for you. So hold on tight and believe in what is to come. Adopt the

---

1. "He was despised and rejected by men; a man of sorrows, and acquainted with grief; and as one from whom men hide their faces he was despised, and we esteemed him not" (Isa. 53:3).

mind-set of Paul the apostle, who wrote, "I consider that the suf-
ferings of this present time are not worth comparing with the glory
that is to be revealed to us" (Rom. 8:18). Paul wants us to root our
minds and our suffering in the fertile soil of God's glory. Our suffer-
ings here, whatever they are, can't hold a candle to the joy that lies
ahead. Paul says, "Don't even bring them to the table."

Why not? Because there's no point to it. This is not like stacking
up Michael Jordan against Lebron James—it's like pitting Michael
against a Chia Pet. The glory of God that's waiting to be revealed
trumps, triumphs over, every tear and pain we feel.

Oh, that we would believe this! It doesn't belittle what we go
through here; rather, it maximizes what we will soon see. For we
were made to see glory. We were made to behold God's undiluted
splendor and be satisfied. We need an excitement for eternity, for
that heavenly city. We will be whisked away into the robust amaz-
ingness of God's goodness. Fully. Finally. Eternally. As the great
theologian Frank Sinatra once crooned, "The best is yet to come."
God will bring us into eternity and lovingly remove all the tears
from our cheeks.

Jonathan Edwards knew this when he
said about our future world, "There can
no such thing as grief enter, to be an allay
to the happiness and joy of that world of
blessedness. Grief is an utter stranger in
that world. God hath promised that he
will wipe away all tears from their eyes, and
there shall be no more sorrow."[2] The deep

> **The deep sadness
> we feel in this
> world won't be able
> to breathe in the
> new earth.**

sadness we feel in this world won't be able to breathe in the new earth,
for Jesus purchased not only our souls but also our indomitable joy

2. Jonathan Edwards, *The Works of Jonathan Edwards*, vol. 2 (Bellingham,
WA: Logos Bible Software, 2008), 208.

in him, and the same hands that took the nails will wipe away our tears. All the sadness and pain you once knew will be forever lifted from your life—for he is going to make *all things* new. The former pains of earth will be done away with, and his love will consume all things—including you.

Don't feel ashamed that some tears remain. Don't feel crushed that you still feel crushed. You aren't a lesser Christian. God expects that he will wipe some tears away when you see him in glory. And he is glad to take them away. He wants to. He longs to. He loves you.

Until that marvelous day arrives, resolve to "set your minds on things that are above, not on things that are on earth. For you have died, and your life is hidden with Christ in God" (Col. 3:2–3). Christian, your life is found in Christ. Set your mind on *him*. Your hope and identity aren't found in tears but in what Jesus has accomplished through his blood. Sulk on the earth no more, but seek what is above. Eternity is around the bend. Faith in him will get you through and he will wipe away every tear. He promises.

What tears still linger on your face?

What pain do you need to bring to the throne?

Are you clinging to his promises?

May this promise of God's love lift you up and get you through whatever has got you down . . .

The LORD is my shepherd; I shall not want.
He makes me lie down in green pastures.
He leads me beside still waters.
He restores my soul.
He leads me in paths of righteousness for his name's sake.
Even though I walk through the valley of the shadow of death,
I will fear no evil, for you are with me;
your rod and your staff, they comfort me.

You prepare a table before me in the presence of my enemies;
you anoint my head with oil; my cup overflows.
Surely goodness and mercy shall follow me all the days of my life,
and I shall dwell in the house of the LORD forever.

PSALM 23

CHAPTER 16

You Are a Gospel Soldier

*The weapons of our warfare are not of the flesh
but have divine power to destroy strongholds.*

2 Corinthians 10:4

Please stop having quiet times. I know this is a devotional book, but it's not meant to be quiet. By all means, read your Bible. Meet with God. Take up your coffee and sit with the Word, but realize this is no *quiet* time.

Twice our Sacred Book calls itself a sword.[1] Swords are not quiet instruments. Swords cut, pierce, defend, kill, and advance loudly. *Clang!* is the sword's soundtrack. A sword is only quiet when it's not being used. It may be quiet as we open the Bible in the wee hours, but what goes on inside us should resemble the Battle of Mordor. Either a battle is raging or a soldier is readying for one.[2] Sheathed swords are quiet, not active ones.

Part of your new identity in Christ is that of a soldier: "Share in suffering as a good soldier of Christ Jesus. No soldier gets entangled in civilian pursuits, since his aim is to please the one who enlisted him" (2 Tim. 2:3–4). You are told to "wage the good warfare" and "fight the good fight" (1 Tim. 1:18; 6:12).

---

1. "For the word of God is living and active, sharper than any two-edged sword, piercing to the division of soul and of spirit, of joints and of marrow, and discerning the thoughts and intentions of the heart" (Heb. 4:12). "Take the helmet of salvation, and the sword of the Spirit, which is the word of God" (Eph. 6:17).
2. "And, as shoes for your feet, having put on the readiness given by the gospel of peace" (Eph. 6:15).

You are a gospel soldier, which means you are a Bible-wielder. Gospel soldiers don't read and memorize Bible verses like a person collecting antique swords; we collect Scripture verses to use them in combat. We build an arsenal because the Enemy prowls (1 Peter 5:8). Since the cosmic forces haven't gone quietly, we train. We wield. We fight.[3]

Imagine the spine of your Bible. Picture grooves, like the handle of a sword, where your hands have been. Envision pages littered with circles, underlines, notes, comments, prayers—signs of use, of a soldier preparing. We war not only against the spirits of the age but also against our "old man," the flesh. A Jesus-exalting life rejects the lameness of our flesh and the sins it pants after.

Christianity's aim is for us to experience new life in the kingdom of Christ, glorifying, exalting, and savoring Jesus. God seeks something far higher than good, clean, normal, comfy, morally upstanding people sitting in a church building on Sunday morning, nodding their heads to another great sermon. He is calling us to greatness in the environment of his grace. We are surrounded by grace, and that grace leads us to fight against our sin. Romans 8:13 is a declaration of all-out war on sin: "If you live according to the flesh you will die, but if by the Spirit you put to death the deeds of the body, you will live." That's personal. "*You* put to death." God is talking right to us.

> **We are surrounded by grace, and that grace leads us to fight against our sin.**

The gospel gives birth to new creatures and freshly enlisted soldiers. Paul reminds us that "though we walk in the flesh, we are not waging war according to the flesh. For the weapons of our warfare

---

3. "For we do not wrestle against flesh and blood, but against the rulers, against the authorities, against the cosmic powers over this present darkness, against the spiritual forces of evil in the heavenly places" (Eph. 6:12).

are not of the flesh but have divine power to destroy strongholds. We destroy arguments and every lofty opinion raised against the knowledge of God, and take every thought captive to obey Christ" (2 Cor. 10:3–5). Killing sin involves more than merely tidying up nasty parts of our lives; it's about decimating and ransacking the enemy. It's a blitzkrieg against the satanic forces' arguments and lofty opinions. Satan has been peddling such garbage since Eden. Boil down the Genesis 3 temptation and you hear, "Take and eat (or *trust*) this created thing over the Creator." That is why in the Lord's Supper, the Creator offers a new meal that says, in effect, "Take and eat (or trust) in me."

As you are reading this book, the cosmic powers are setting up their tent and hawking their high-sounding lies against God and his gospel. Here is how you fight: take every thought captive to obey Jesus. We war against our sin because we want to obey Jesus—not to be saved by him, but because we *are* saved by him. It is never legalistic to want to obey Jesus. It's stupid not to. The flesh is stupid. Tune it out. We don't manage sin—we can't; we've tried. We massacre it.

> We war against our sin because we want to obey Jesus – not to be saved by him, but because we *are* saved by him.

The Bible says we're to "make no provision for the flesh." That's because if we give the flesh an inch, it'll take the West Coast. Sin wants to reach its utmost potential. Anger wants to become murder; bitterness wants to sprout divorce; a glance wants to become adultery. So we fight, not with new tactics but with old truth. With *the* truth. With weaponized gospel power. "The gospel," as Ray Ortlund once said, "is kryptonite against our sins." The more our souls are rattled by the awesomeness of the gospel, the less we are drawn to sin.

When you believe that Jesus really died for *your* sins, rose again for you, counts you free, is alive for you and in you, loves you even in the light of all your sins, and is thrilled to call you his brother or sister, then sin looks quite lame. Yuck.

So when the dark spirits attack your identity in Christ or question God's love for a wretch like you, your battle cry is simple: "Abba! Father!" That's gospel power. The sonic boom of the gospel flattens our sins. Grace is *that* powerful. Grace abounds to wipe out our sins. Christians aren't sinless—we will still struggle in this war. But the gospel is still good news for Christians: we are forgiven. That's a key component of the sword of the Spirit; don't go into battle without it.

Oddly, some people argue against daily Bible reading. I understand why: they oppose legalism. That's good. Grace-addicted lives want nothing to do with legalism. However, I think we don't understand legalism, or maybe we misdiagnose it. Legalism is a bogus attempt to earn right standing before God. In legalism, justification is pursued by means other than Christ alone—works, good deeds, and other religious hoops for us to jump through. That's legalism: striving for righteousness *apart* from the person and work of Jesus and the indwelling presence of the Holy Spirit. But the gospel isn't a merit system; rather, it *empowers* us for holiness.

Encouraging daily Bible reading isn't legalism. (Encouraging anything isn't a yoke. It's encouragement, not a Nazi bulletin.) If you miss a day or two, OK. No finger-wagging, no courtroom, no condemnation. But there's a difference between liberty and apathy. Christians who have full access to the Bible, as we do in the United States, ought to be in it as much as possible—dare I say, daily. We will not grow without it (1 Peter 2:2). It's not legalistic to say so; that's just the way it is.

If the apostle Paul were around today, I wonder how often he'd be taking in the completed sixty-six books of the Bible. The writer of Hebrews tells us to imitate the faith of our leaders (Heb. 13:7). Think of your favorite pastor, preacher, author, or figure from church history, then gauge their Bible intake and copy it.

In Proverbs 8, wisdom is personified as a woman who calls out, "Blessed is the one who listens to me, *watching daily at my gates, waiting beside my doors*. For whoever finds me finds life and obtains favor from the LORD, but he who fails to find me injures himself; all who hate me love death" (Prov. 8:34–36, italics mine).

Daily. *Daily*.

We are blessed by looking for wisdom, by watching and waiting outside her door. Wisdom's gates are the covers of our Bible.

> **We are blessed by looking for wisdom, by watching and waiting outside her door.**

Fling them open, read, and pray, "God, I'm here. Wisdom? Hello? I'm looking for you. Change me. Be glorified, God." There in the Word we find "Christ Jesus, who became to us wisdom from God" (1 Cor. 1:30). Jesus is more than wise; he *is* wisdom. Who cares about pithy statements. We need the power of Jesus Christ. We need the mega-wise Man of God, the Son of Man, the great I Am, to instruct us. How often do you need him? How often do you need to learn from him? I know my answer: daily. Seems like a good thing to me. A life that is heaven-bent on exalting Jesus will be committed to the Bible, because we believe our Lord when he said, "If you abide in my word, you are truly my disciples, and you will know the truth, and the truth will set you free" (John 8:31–32).

Read the Word, memorize the Word, and meditate on the Word to become quick and adept at wielding its razor-edged blade. Our hearts should be filled with the echoing screeches of the old man and his little hobgoblins, our indwelling sins. The sword of the Spirit takes no prisoners. It cuts through the thoughts and intentions of the heart. It calls the bluff. It swacks through our fig leaves and shows what lies behind their covering: our deceptions, phoniness, self-righteousness—whatever it is within us that requires the gospel of grace. The sword of God's Word reverberates throughout our entire life. Nuclear bombs envy its force.

Along with your morning cuppa joe, pick up the Word to meet with the King and enjoy his reign and rule. Listen for the Lion of Judah's roar. Then put down your coffee, walk out into the world, and say, "Long live the King!"[4]

May you have an intentional time with the Word—and may it be anything but quiet. May the Word resound through your soul.

Fight the good fight of the faith. Take hold of the eternal life to which you were called and about which you made the good confession in the presence of many witnesses.

1 Timothy 6:12

---

4. "To the King of the ages, immortal, invisible, the only God, be honor and glory forever and ever. Amen" (1 Tim. 1:17).

CHAPTER 17

You Are Condemnation-Free

There is therefore now no condemnation
for those who are in Christ Jesus.

ROMANS 8:1

I don't know of a more supercharged verse than Romans 8:1. Let this one stay in repeat-mode in your heart. We struggle, flounder, disappoint others (and ourselves), and end up thinking we are losers—or worse, that we are in trouble with God. Maybe he doesn't love us as much, especially if we did *that* sin *again*—right?

Wrong. Way wrong.

The gospel is now the banner over your life, and it reads Not Condemned!

> **The gospel is now the banner over your life, and it reads Not Condemned!**

Today there are all kinds of gluten-free products. Even some makers of bottled water want to assure you that their water contains no gluten. But gluten-free doesn't mean "zero gluten present." The Food and Drug Administration says a food can be classified gluten-free as long as it contains less than twenty-two parts per million of gluten. (That's a very small amount. It's the lowest amount that can be detected with our twenty-first-century gadgets and gizmos.)

But while such not-quite-pure purity standards may fly in the world, they don't in the kingdom of Christ. The good news of the gospel is that not even a trace of condemnation toward you remains. Your identity is in Christ, and you are therefore labeled "condemnation-free"—declared so by God, whose all-seeing eye detects even the minutest impurities. You are fully forgiven of all your cosmic crimes. Your treason against the King of kings has been wiped from your record because the King himself took all of the charges and was punished in your place. The sins you are most ashamed of, the ones that knot your stomach as you think of them—Jesus died for them all, and now God says, "Don't you dare feel condemned any longer. I love you. My Son has cleansed you. Forever." You are justified, legally righteous, because of Jesus—and not only that, but you are also adopted. Justification is a great grace, and to be adopted into God's family is a grace upon grace. Yet that's all he ever gives his children—matchless, infinite, marvelous grace.

You need Romans 8:1 in your back pocket, because condemnation will rear its ugly face at any given moment. Satan's forces prowl the earth, and they will try to smother your joy and hem you in to a guilt-driven existence. But Romans 8:1 can serve as Kevlar against the devil's fiery potshots.

God loves you so much! He wants you to feel it. He cares for you. All he gives you is grace. He didn't save you so you could hang your head and feel guilty—that's not what he wants for you. He wants you to experience freedom, joy, and a life centered on the gospel.

Our God is not like the bizarre gods of this world. Getting a false god's attention must be difficult. Have you seen what some religions require? Weird clothes, improv dance-offs, oddly placed piercings, the consumption of unsanitary foods—yeesh. Adherents of some false religions perform certain mantras and incantations in order to get their god's attention, as if dialing in a special formula will score divine dealings. Worshipers of false gods labor under the tyranny of performance.

But too many Christians labor just as hard under the slave

master of legalism, and Jesus wants you to be liberated from that stink. He said, "When you pray, do not heap up empty phrases as the Gentiles do, for they think that they will be heard for their many words" (Matt. 6:7). Jesus demolishes the idea of having to pique God's interest with "many words." If you are a Christian, you don't have to do anything to pique his interest in you. He was interested in you before the foundation of the world, and he still is.[1]

The Father is eager to hear from you. He is game to help. He is on call. There are no hoops or red tape; you have all you need and are qualified to approach the throne of grace. You are a child of God. You don't have to perform an evangelical rain dance with the right amount of Bible reading, prayer, Christian music, missional living, fasting, and podcasting to earn God's interest. It's yours in Christ. "The eyes of the LORD are toward the righteous and his ears toward their cry" (Ps. 34:15). You are never off his radar. God's mighty hand of love is on you at all times.[2] The Father of Lights knows and cares when a bird drops—and *you* are more valuable than a Manhattan pigeon. You don't have to pull off feats of superhero spirituality to earn God's help and care. In reality, he's already helping. He upholds the entire universe, and that includes you.[3]

God is constantly interested and invested in you. The wonder of God's grace is that even when you aren't interested in God, he is still for you. We tend to think that God will treat us the way we treat him. We couldn't be more wrong. When we are unfaithful, he

1. "He chose us in [Christ] before the foundation of the world, that we should be holy and blameless before him. In love he predestined us for adoption as sons through Jesus Christ, according to the purpose of his will" (Eph. 1:4–5).
2. "I give them eternal life, and they will never perish, and no one will snatch them out of my hand. My Father, who has given them to me, is greater than all, and no one is able to snatch them out of the Father's hand" (John 10:28–29).
3. "He is the radiance of the glory of God and the exact imprint of his nature, and he upholds the universe by the word of his power. After making purification for sins, he sat down at the right hand of the Majesty on high" (Heb. 1:3).

remains faithful.[4] When we aren't interested, he still is. And he will woo us back with more of himself. He will draw us back with more grace and love.

Now, don't miss this next part.

God loves his children, but that doesn't mean he approves of everything we do. Grace isn't a punch card; it's a

> The wonder of God's grace is that even when you aren't interested in God, he is still for you.

cross. Like all children, we will disobey our Father, and like a good father, he will discipline us. This too is grace. "Those whom I love, I reprove and discipline, so be zealous and repent" (Rev. 3:19). It's the unloving parent who smiles at the stupidity and rebellion of their kids: "Whoever spares the rod hates his son, but he who loves him is diligent to discipline him" (Prov. 13:24). You'd better believe God is diligent to sanctify us into the image of his beloved Son.

God's love for you is so zealous that he doesn't mind making you uncomfortable. He won't let you be at ease in sin. When a Christian wallows in slop, it's not long until God's steel-toed love brings a wake-up call. God loves his children by correcting them. He will convict and correct you with the Word, he'll rebuke you in community, and he will let your sin be found out—all because he loves you.

Gospel-centered hearts don't see God's discipline as unloving or as an erosion of relationship. Just the opposite: it is a revealing of love and a demonstration of relationship. Our Father's discipline is never a divine *tsk-tsk, shame on you*, or God getting back at us for the dumb stuff we've dabbled in. Rather, it's him saying, "I love you and I'm going to help you." God will always be for you—but he will never be for your sin. His discipline is more than a divine hand-slap: it's an education, a moment of discipleship. You are meant to

---

4. "If we are faithless, he remains faithful—for he cannot deny himself" (2 Tim. 2:13).

learn from the experience. God is educating you on grace—that you are still accepted because of Jesus' righteousness and not yours. He shows that he still loves the messed up, sinful you.

In Revelation 3:19, John says that out of love, God will discipline us, so be eager to change. Don't fight God in the process. (You can, but it's pointless.) Don't kick against the goads of love. When you resist change, refusing to repent, and are slow to admit sin, then you are refusing the love of God. He wants to bring you back to your first love.[5]

Accepting discipline, correction, and rebuke comes back to the gospel. Do you believe that God loves you—even though you aren't perfect? Do you trust that God does what is good for you, even if it means outing your sin in your small group?

And do you have unconfessed sin because you don't want to face the stone-cold truth that you aren't as great as you think you are? Do you not want others to see the real you? If these describe you, believe the gospel yet again: you are counted righteous in Christ *alone*. Be eager to repent. Receive discipline as a gift of the gospel.

> The same love that saved you is the love that sanctifies you.

The same love that saved you is the love that sanctifies you. God loves sinners, and he loves to change sinners. Praise God for his great love for you.

Odds are I don't know you, but I know you are a sinner like me. I know you need grace like me. I don't know where you are, or what you've done, or what you are carrying on your shoulders—but God does. He knows sins you are going to commit that you don't even know about. And he tells you, "In my Son, you are cleared today and you'll be cleared tomorrow." There is nothing that could

---

5. "But I have this against you, that you have abandoned the love you had at first. Remember therefore from where you have fallen; repent, and do the works you did at first. If not, I will come to you and remove your lampstand from its place, unless you repent" (Rev. 2:4–5).

be revealed about your life that hasn't already been cleansed by the blood of the Galilean. In Jesus, your future sins are already in the past. Tomorrow's failure has been postdated to A.D. 33. That's glad tidings and the glory of the gospel.

May you rejoice in the Lord today. Believe and live like there is now no condemnation for you in Christ Jesus. God's love is that strong.

"I will sprinkle clean water on you, and you shall be clean from all your uncleannesses, and from all your idols I will cleanse you."

EZEKIEL 36:25

CHAPTER 18

A Gospel-Centered Catechism

What then shall we say to these things?

Romans 8:31

Catechizing believers—teaching a list of questions and answers—is a deeply rooted practice of the bride of Christ. It has been tucked away in the attic of church life, but it's coming back. Though dusty, we can recover it. Catechism is a powerful, helpful, biblical method of teaching others—and yourself.

The Westminster and Heidelberg catechisms are two well-known, time-honored catechisms. Let's sample three questions from them to see how helpful these catechisms are.

From the Westminster Catechism

Question 1: What is the chief end of man?

Answer: Man's chief end is to glorify God, and to enjoy him forever.

Question 4: What is God?

Answer: God is a Spirit, infinite, eternal, and unchangeable, in his being, wisdom, power, holiness, justice, goodness, and truth.

From the Heidelberg Catechism

Question 1: What is thy only comfort in life and death?

Answer: That I with body and soul, both in life and death, am not my own, but belong unto my faithful Saviour Jesus Christ; who, with his precious blood, has fully satisfied for all my sins, and delivered me from all the power of the devil; and so preserves me that without the will of my heavenly Father, not a hair can fall from my head; yea, that all things must be subservient to my salvation, and therefore, by his Holy Spirit, he also assures me of eternal life, and makes me sincerely willing and ready, henceforth, to live unto him.

We need to become experts in the art of preaching the gospel to ourselves. One of the greatest thinkers and pastors of the last hundred years was Martyn Lloyd-Jones, referred to by many as "The Doctor." Lloyd-Jones rightly diagnosed why so many Christians flounder in their daily lives and experiences with God. The Doctor said, "Have you realized that most of your unhappiness in life is due to the fact that you are listening to yourself instead of talking to yourself?"[1]

> **We need to become experts in the art of preaching the gospel to ourselves.**

He's so right. A defeated, depressed, downtrodden, exasperated, exhausted, joyless, burned-out Christianity is not Christianity. We need to lay hold of the cross and remember our new life in Christ. We need to preach the gospel to ourselves.

---

1. Martyn Lloyd-Jones, *Spiritual Depression: Its Causes and Cures* (Grand Rapids: Eerdmans, 1965), 20.

Lloyd-Jones again: "The main art in the matter of spiritual living is to know how to handle yourself. You have to take yourself in hand, you have to address yourself, preach to yourself, question yourself."[2] We need to *catechize* ourselves. Catechisms are a turnkey help in the practice of preaching to ourselves. Catechism ought to be in our spiritual discipline tool chest.

The long-tested spiritual disciplines need a freshening in our perspectives. What can often be seen as a quiet and cute time around a cup of coffee, journal, study Bible, assorted pens and highlighters—maybe some instrumental music—is nothing short of kingdom warfare. We don't read the Bible to get a pick-me-up; we read to grow in the knowledge of the holy—yes, and amen!—and we take up the spiritual disciplines as weaponry against the ancient Reptile and his lackeys. "For the weapons of our warfare are not of the flesh but have divine power to destroy strongholds. We destroy arguments and every lofty opinion raised against the knowledge of God, and take every thought captive to obey Christ" (2 Cor. 10:4–5).

> The last thing Satan wants is for the church to obey Jesus, glorify Jesus, honor Jesus, and spread the fame of Jesus – and that should be our first thing, the chief aim of all spiritual disciplines.

The last thing Satan wants is for the church to obey Jesus, glorify Jesus, honor Jesus, and spread the fame of Jesus—and that should be our first thing, the chief aim of all spiritual disciplines.

When you hear the hiss of accusation and doubt, and when fiery arrows fly toward you, Paul's catechism of victory in Romans 8:31–39 is your protection; and if you resist the devil and draw near to God, the snake will bolt (James 4:7–8).

As you read Romans 8:31–39, look for the question marks:

---

2. Ibid., 21.

What then shall we say to these things? If God is for us, who can be against us? He who did not spare his own Son but gave him up for us all, how will he not also with him graciously give us all things? Who shall bring any charge against God's elect? It is God who justifies. Who is to condemn? Christ Jesus is the one who died—more than that, who was raised—who is at the right hand of God, who indeed is interceding for us. Who shall separate us from the love of Christ? Shall tribulation, or distress, or persecution, or famine, or nakedness, or danger, or sword? As it is written,

"For your sake we are being killed all the day long;
    we are regarded as sheep to be slaughtered."

No, in all these things we are more than conquerors through him who loved us. For I am sure that neither death nor life, nor angels nor rulers, nor things present nor things to come, nor powers, nor height nor depth, nor anything else in all creation, will be able to separate us from the love of God in Christ Jesus our Lord.

What you've just read may be one of the first Christian catechisms. Paul sets up seven questions (in ten verses) and gives the answers. What is he doing? He is catechizing us. His seven questions can be distilled into four main questions:

Question 1: Why should I not doubt God's love and care for me? (vv. 31–32)

Answer: If God is for us, who can be against us? He who did not spare his own Son but gave him up for us all, how will he not also with him graciously give us all things?

Question 2: How come charges will not stand against me? (v. 33)

Answer: It is God who justifies.

Question 3: Can I ever be condemned? (v. 34)

Answer: Christ Jesus is the one who died—more than that, who was raised—who is at the right hand of God, who indeed is interceding for us.

Question 4: Can anything separate me from the love of Christ? Will I ever be unloved by God? (vv. 37–39)

Answer: No, in all these things we are more than conquerors through him who loved us. For I am sure that neither death nor life, nor angels nor rulers, nor things present nor things to come, nor powers, nor height nor depth, nor anything else in all creation, will be able to separate us from the love of God in Christ Jesus our Lord.

Paul is giving us a gospel-centered catechism. The questions are helpful, but the answers are the weapon we need. What weapon does Paul give when we fear condemnation? Read our Bible more? Pray harder? None of these. Stand-alone spiritual disciplines are just vehicles that help us draw near to God. They aren't the answer to a struggling heart; rather, they take us to the answer. Each question is answered with a gospel treasure. And it always comes back to God's love.

The Romans 8 passage lauds God's love four times in three verses (vv. 35, 37, 39). That love is made plain and clear in the gospel: "For while we were still weak, at the right time Christ died for the ungodly. For one will scarcely die for a righteous person—though perhaps for a good person one would dare even to die—but God shows his love for us in that while we were still sinners, Christ died for us" (Rom. 5:6–8).

God wants you to know and feel his love. Why else frame every answer with it? You can never feel too loved by God. Are you sure of his love? That's the point of the catechism: to be sure. Preach to yourself the immeasurable, matchless bounty of God's love for you. Here is a responsive reading, based on Romans 8:31–39, that can assist you in catechizing yourself with the gospel.

A Responsive Reading

I struggle to believe God's love and care for me. Is there hope?

God is for me. No one can stand against God's plan for me. He didn't spare his Son but gave him up for us all, and that includes me. So how will he not also with him graciously give me all things?

Is it true that God won't cast me aside? I've done some bad things; I'll never be good enough.

No one can condemn me, for Jesus died in my place. More than that, he is alive—and he reigns over my life and is interceding for me.

My life is heavy; things aren't going as I planned. I thought God loved me.

Nothing can separate me from God's love. Trouble, distress, persecution, poverty, danger, and death cannot remove me from God's grace. In all these things, I am more than a conqueror through him who loved me.

Satan prowls around me. I've sinned too much. I've sinned too big. I'm nervous about my future.

I am sure that neither death nor life, nor angels nor rulers, nor things present nor things to come, nor powers,
nor height nor depth, nor anything else in all creation,
will be able to separate me from the love of God in Christ
Jesus my Lord.

I confess these truths, clinging to Jesus—I believe and live again.

Christ be praised.

PART FOUR

What Is Gospel Community?

Gospel community is a group of Christians encouraging and exhorting each other to walk in a manner worthy of the gospel of Christ.

Gospel community is the people of God living out the gospel ethics of the kingdom of God.

CHAPTER 19

Everyone a Gospeler

*Let us hold fast the confession of our hope without wavering,
for he who promised is faithful. And let us consider how to
stir up one another to love and good works, not neglecting to
meet together, as is the habit of some, but encouraging one
another, and all the more as you see the Day drawing near.*

HEBREWS 10:23–25

Preaching the gospel isn't only for preachers. Every Christian is a gospeler.

Gospeler is an actual word; it means "a person who zealously teaches or professes faith in the gospel." In the Christian community, everyone is a gospeler. Mr. Webster's dictionary describes the sound of a gospel community—people teaching each other the gospel. We never move on from the gospel. The good news isn't only the diving board into Christianity—it's also the pool. And gospel community is a pool party.

In Hebrews 10, the author pleads with a group of Christians to "hold fast the confession of our hope." What confession? The one of hope:

> If you *confess* with your mouth that Jesus is Lord and believe in your heart that God raised him from the dead, you will be saved. (Rom. 10:9, italics mine)

> Therefore God has highly exalted him and bestowed on him the name that is above every name, so that at

the name of Jesus every knee should bow, in heaven
and on earth and under the earth, and every tongue
confess that Jesus Christ is Lord, to the glory of God
the Father. (Phil. 2:9–11)

The community holds a gospel confession and cannot be lost,
taken for granted, or marginalized.[1] Due to our sinful nature, we
gradually drift, like an anchorless boat, away from the safety of the center. But gospel community fights the drift.

The community holds a gospel confession and cannot be lost, taken for granted, or marginalized.

Hebrews 10:24 shows why a gospel-centered community is vital: it will "stir up one another to love and good works." When the love of Christ is central, it resurrects a one-another-ness in the community. When people are honest about who they are and firmly believe that Christ alone and none of their works makes them righteous before God, then everything changes. Everything and everyone.

The gospel shakes things up in a good way. It spurs on the lollygaggers. Groggy hearts are reawakened to the power of the gospel. Sleep in the corner of the eyes gets wiped away. Gospel community is a living and breathing picture of the gospel. It convinces the skeptics; it is a powerful apologetic for the gospel.[2] The world hasn't seen anything like it.

Love creates commitment to a group of people, to a church, and to gospel friends. When Hebrews 10:24 happens, verse 25 is the natural outcome: "Not neglecting to meet together, as is the habit

---

1. "By their approval of this service, they will glorify God because of your submission that comes from your confession of the gospel of Christ, and the generosity of your contribution for them and for all others" (2 Cor. 9:13).

2. "By this all people will know that you are my disciples, if you have love for one another" (John 13:35).

of some, but encouraging one another, and all the more as you see the Day drawing near." Gospel-centered Christians don't neglect the souls of others. They want to be a source of encouragement, and they know that they themselves need to be encouraged. And there is no better encouragement than the gospel.

Every truth from the gospel is like a bunker-busting missile. It crashes through the hard outer shells of discouraged, floundering, and wandering hearts and releases the explosive joy of Christ inside them. When you aren't preaching the gospel to yourself, you need another gospeler to take the mic and encourage you. And then you need to pick up the mic and sing a round of psalms, hymns, and spiritual songs to a friend.[3] A gospel community is about serving and being served, encouraging and being encouraged to find our absolute hope and satisfaction in the risen Jesus.

This can't be overstressed. We are too prone to wander apart from gospel community. Do you know how many days it takes for a heart to harden? One. That's why Hebrews 3:13 tells us to "exhort one another every day, as long as it is called 'today,' that none of you may be hardened by the deceitfulness of sin." The heart is a serious matter. To fend off heart disease, the Bible calls you to a community, one that will be honest with you about your sins.

> You need other Christians who are willing to say the hard things, ones who are ready to speak the truth in love. Do you have them?

I'm not talking about an hour-a-week Bible study; your community must have more roaming privileges. You need people who aren't fenced in, friends who have the right to speak into your life at any time about anything. You need

---

3. "Let the word of Christ dwell in you richly, teaching and admonishing one another in all wisdom, singing psalms and hymns and spiritual songs, with thankfulness in your hearts to God" (Col. 3:16).

other Christians who are willing to say the hard things, ones who are ready to speak the truth in love. Do you have them?

We need exhorting, which literally means, "coming alongside"—all for the express purpose of genuine help. We need to be reined in from time to time; we need to heed our blind spots before we crash the car. Sheep wander and roam, and without a loving redirection they may eventually drift into desiring sin more than desiring God. But an honest-to-goodness gospel community will fight sin together. Real community is a preemptive strike against a hard heart.

Do you have this kind of community? Do you think you can do this alone? No one can. And as a pastor, it is my experience that most Christians don't live this way. They think they can lone-ranger it. Way wrong. Is that you?

Are you trying to hide something? Are you too ashamed to talk about it? Are you worried about what others will think if you open up to them? The Bible says, "There is no fear in love, but perfect love casts out fear. For fear has to do with punishment, and whoever fears has not been perfected in love" (1 John 4:18). The love of God—for sinners like us—smashes the fear of man.

But if you are still a slave to approval, pride will rule your life, not the power of Christ. Arrogant people aren't the only proud ones; pride also wishes it had something to be arrogant about. Pride can puff itself up in community and pride can hide from community. It will keep you from reaping the benefits of biblical, Jesus-exalting, gospel-loving, truly helpful connection with others, and it will cause you to drift. A hardening heart grows colder under the darkness of pride; sin grows exponentially under pride's reign. You need gospel truth to reign over you, for Jesus died to set you free.[4]

The gospel frees you from living for the approval of others,

---

4. "For freedom Christ has set us free; stand firm therefore, and do not submit again to a yoke of slavery" (Gal. 5:1).

because you've been fully approved by
God in Christ. You don't have to impress
anyone or justify your acceptance in the
group, because Jesus has already justified
you and your name is written in the Book
of Life. You don't have to be paralyzingly
ashamed of your sin, because everyone else
is a sinner too. The gospel levels the playing field, because the only perfect one is

**The gospel frees you
from living for the
approval of others,
because you've been
fully approved by
God in Christ.**

Jesus. God already knows about the sludge in your heart, and he
loves you just the same. Nothing liberates like the gospel.

So go alongside others and have others come alongside you.
Pursue their fellowship. Invite it. Gospel-centered friends help each
other war against sin. If you don't have a gospel community, find
one, and don't wait to be real about the state of your soul. Enjoy
the gifts of the brothers and sisters in Christ. You need them more
than you think.

May you walk in the light with a gospel community, in the
power of the gospel, for the glory of God.

*Bear one another's burdens,
and so fulfill the law of Christ.*

GALATIANS 6:2

CHAPTER 20

A Community of Gospel Friends

A man of many companions may come to ruin,
but there is a friend who sticks closer than a brother.

PROVERBS 18:24

God has a massive vision for your life. Whatever plan you have, God's is much bigger—and better. If you are in Christ, God has promised to make your heart and life resemble Jesus Christ.[1] The image of Christ is your destiny. That's a sight for sore souls.

Consider Jesus. He is zealous and tender. Service, compassion, humility, and honesty aren't foreign to him. Crowds don't make him nervous, and he loves the quiet place. He is the Light of the World, and like light, he is pure, bright, and open. Jesus is *real*. You can trust Jesus. He isn't shady; there is nothing fishy about Jesus of Nazareth.

All of this matters because, as 1 John 1:7 says, we are to "walk in the light, as he is in the light." Gospel freedom ignites a new lifestyle, one of light. Gospel-powered lives are bright and open, not dark and dingy like the spot between a dumpster and the wall. People *could* get back there, but who would want to? It's shadowy, grimy, and uninviting; you have no idea what you are dealing with back there. That's not light-living. Light invites. Walking in the light stimulates and pursues community.

---

1. "Those whom he foreknew he also predestined to be conformed to the image of his Son" (Rom. 8:29).

Walking with God will always lead to walking with others. As John says, "We have fellowship with one another" (v. 7). True fellowship with God will involve true community with God's people, a fellowship of light in the gospel. Dark community is the dumpster-to-wall style of community: You are there but not open for community, available but distant. You can be in a group of Christians and sit mere inches away from each other but still choose to be light years apart. This happens when you aren't walking in the light of his light but under another source. Whether it's legalism, self-righteousness, "I'm okay"-ness, or comparing yourself to others, anything other than the light of Christ is a condemning black light. It offers zero help and will keep you from the true light.

When walking in the light of Christ, you won't be concerned about being judged. You already know your verdict: justified. Walking in the light means you

> **Walking with God will always lead to walking with others.**

are walking in Christ, the Light of the World, and the fear of man is pushed out. Your sin and flesh are nocturnal creatures; they can't hang around while the ten-trillion-watt Light of the World beams on you. Anxiety scurries like a cockroach. Sins lose their hiding places; the gospel empowers you to toss your struggles with sin into the open, knowing that you are forgiven by God and secure in Christ, and you can ask for the fellowship of light to accompany you on a dragon slaying journey. You do this in the bright light of community because you know that "if we say we have no sin, we deceive ourselves, and the truth is not in us. If we confess our sins, he is faithful and just to forgive us our sins and to cleanse us from all unrighteousness" (1 John 1:8–9). The gospel gives you the best friends this world has ever seen.

All of us need Bible-believing, sin-identifying, soul-caring, Jesus-exalting friends. Those with whom we will be honest will be honest with us. We need our bluffs called. Yes-friends are no friends. Sins need to be graciously pointed out and carried to the woodshed together. We need real friends, gospel friends, homeboys and homegirls who give good news before good advice. Friends who remind us of God's grace—*that's* real community.

> A gospel culture is one where no sin is safe but sinners are always welcome.

A gospel culture is one where no sin is safe but sinners are always welcome. Many have been flogged and flayed by others in the name of truth. That's not the gospel of grace. When sin is confessed and a sinner is looking for help, the gospel doesn't burn people at the stake—it gives hope. Jesus goes the distance with sinners who want to change. Isn't he doing that right now for you and me?

If you aren't sold on community, it's probably because you've been bamboozled by *companions*. We don't need more companions or affinity-based "friends"; those relationships are built on sand. When the storm comes, they aren't built high enough to handle real life. But biblical friends—gospel-giving, life-breathing, burden-bearing friends—can weather the storm. They'll keep us from hitting bottom.

A gospel friend "loves at all times, and a brother is born for adversity" (Prov. 17:17). Naomi had a real friend in Ruth.[2] A real friend is self-sacrificing. In the words of Jesus, "Greater love has no one than this, that someone lay down his life for his friends. You are my friends if you do what I command you. No longer do I call you servants, for the servant does not know what his master is doing; but I have called you friends, for all that I have heard from my Father I have made known to you" (John 15:13–15).

---

2. "[Naomi] said, 'See, your sister-in-law has gone back to her people and to her gods; return after your sister-in-law.' But Ruth said, 'Do not urge me to leave you or to return from following you. For where you go I will go, and where you lodge I will lodge. Your people shall be my people, and your God my God. Where you die I will die, and there will I be buried. May the LORD do so to me and more also if anything but death parts me from you.' And when Naomi saw that she was determined to go with her, she said no more" (Ruth 1:15–18).

Gospel-soaked friends don't bail at the first riff or tiff. They don't ignore us when times are shaky. Jesus, the friend who sticks closer than a flesh-born brother, has promised, "I am with you always, to the end of the age" (Matt. 28:20), and gospel friends mirror his loyalty.

Humility, grace, and self-sacrifice dominate friendships fueled by the gospel. Friendships flounder when we think of ourselves more highly than we ought.[3] Gospel-driven friends look to the interests of others, because this is the mind of Christ, which is now theirs as well.[4]

By the power of Jesus, be a gospel friend. And may you have heaps of gospel friends in return. Pray for these friends. Who do you need to call?

Today, may you walk in the brightness of Christ—in the light as he is in the light and *is* the Light. In the beams of his grace, may you feel the warmth of God's love.

This is the message we have heard from him and proclaim to you, that God is light, and in him is no darkness at all. If we say we have fellowship with him while we walk in darkness, we lie and do not practice the truth. But if we walk in the light, as he is in the light, we have fellowship with one another.

1 JOHN 1:5–7

---

3. "By the grace given to me I say to everyone among you not to think of himself more highly than he ought to think" (Rom. 12:3).

4. "Let each of you look not only to his own interests, but also to the interests of others. Have this mind among yourselves, which is yours in Christ Jesus" (Phil. 2:4–5).

CHAPTER 21

Jesus Loves the Church. Do You?

Falling to the ground he heard a voice saying to him, "Saul, Saul, why are you persecuting me?"

ACTS 9:4

The apostle Paul's testimony is amazing. The Lord Jesus met him on the road and caused him to be born again. There aren't many people in the world who can say, "Well, Jesus showed up physically and *everything* changed." Even Paul's name changed.

Paul's testimony reveals a powerful truth about how we should view the church, the body of Christ. Jesus asked Paul, "Why are you persecuting me?"

"Me"? In Acts 1, Jesus went back to heaven; Paul never laid a hand on Jesus. What is Jesus saying? He's telling Paul that whatever is done to the church is also done to Jesus. Christ loves his church so much that he identifies with her completely. Thus, by persecuting Christians, Paul was persecuting Jesus himself.

You cannot separate Jesus from his church. We—the church, his bride—are united with Jesus. Inseparable. Jesus loves the church more than we can imagine.

So how much do *you* love the church? We are about to get all kinds of personal.

I'm passionate about the church, and not only because I'm a pastor. I love the church because Jesus does. How much do you care about the church? Are you connected to the church? Are you faithful to a local church? Jesus shed his blood for the church and never takes her lightly—nor should you (Acts 20:28).

So how involved are you? How connected are you? Fringe? Once-a-monther? C'mon. Some people aren't able to regularly attend their church's gatherings because of health reasons, their work schedule, and so on. But do you miss because you are just too tuckered out? Do you and your kids' hobbies keep you away? The early church braved the sword to gather with God's people, and Christians in our day will hardly brave the rain. That's a problem—one that's bigger than church attendance. This is a love-for-Jesus problem. How we treat his bride equals how we treat him.

How much do you pray for your church? How much do you pray for Jesus to be glorified in the church? Jesus doesn't treat the church like a side item. He loves the church as himself. Jesus and his church cannot be divorced, and your commitment to a church shows a lot about your walk with Jesus. Are you divorced from the church? Come back to the gospel and follow it to a church. You were made to be with God's people. A foot was made for a leg; a thumbnail needs a thumb. Jesus puts other Christians in your life for your benefit, and you for theirs. The Christian faith is no private enterprise. We aren't intended to pursue Jesus alone.

> **The Christian faith is no private enterprise. We aren't intended to pursue Jesus alone.**

Part of your calling as a Christian is to refresh the hearts of your brothers and sisters. We help others follow Jesus by our own vibrant walk with Christ. Gospel-centered Christians are refreshing to be around.

In his letter to Philemon, the apostle Paul asks Philemon to welcome back Onesimus, a runaway slave who left Philemon's house as a pagan but is coming back a believer. Paul requests that Philemon erase all of the wrongs that have been committed against him by

Onesimus and welcome him as a brother in Christ. Paul asks Philemon to live out his Christian faith in a real way, in an act of kindness
that will send shockwaves through the church, community, and
city. Everyone will see Philemon's amazing act of grace, and Paul
knows it will rock them in a momentous way. Because forgiveness
is jaw-dropping. Grace refreshes. Love revives. Kindness energizes.
Acceptance is awe-inducing. Integrity inspires. And in every way,
gospel-centered living invigorates.

"Yes, brother, I want some benefit from you in the Lord," writes
Paul. "Refresh my heart in Christ" (Philem. 1:20).

Paul wants Philemon to live out his gospel doctrine. Talk the
talk *and* walk the walk. "Let your manner of life be worthy of the
gospel of Christ" (Phil. 1:27). That includes your relationship with
the church. If you claim Christ, claim Christ's people. Because we
need each other.

A Christian walking in the power of the Holy Spirit will blow
away the cobwebs of stagnancy and fortify the faithful. Your obedience to Jesus has greater implications than you ever dreamed. Your
walk is divinely designed to urge others along.

God has pre-wired us to be a source of refreshment to one
another. Our faith in action is meant to remind each other of Jesus'
lordship and love, and of the fact that we are forgiven, empowered,
and called to something great. Follow Jesus and encourage others to
do the same. Surround yourself with those who refresh your faith,
because rust doesn't take long to gather on the heart.

Gospel-centered folk are committed church folk. Passion for
the gospel means you have staked your life in everything the gospel
purchased—including the church. If you have a lousy love for the
church, study the gospel. The cross is the testimony of God's love
for you *and* his church. Jesus died for the church; should you love
her any less?

Maybe you've been burned by church people before. I'm sorry.
A true church, a gospel church, should be one of the kindest places

in the universe. If you've been hurt by a church—you confessed a sin and were treated harshly; or you tried to be a part of the church, really tried, but no one ever welcomed you; or the leaders at your last church were corrupt—then know this: Jesus hasn't done you wrong. It's others, including you and me, who are sinful. In a sense, every church is filled with micro-hypocrites, and we all need the

> A true church, a gospel church, should be one of the kindest places in the universe.

risen Jesus. He is the only perfect one. And he wants you to be in fellowship with other believers, so trust him. Look for a gospel-centered church in your community.[1]

Don't let a bad experience rob you of a glorious future. Obey the word of Christ and don't neglect the gathering of his people (Heb. 10:24–25). I've had bad eggs before; they had so much salt the Dead Sea got jealous. Did that stop me from eating eggs again? No way. Commit to Christ and his people, as Paul counsels in Romans 12:4–5: "For as in one body we have many members, and the members do not all have the same function, so we, though many, are one body in Christ, and individually members one of another."

If you like the church but think lightly of her—repent. Think of her the way Jesus does. It's his body, of which you are a part. If you love the church, ask Jesus to help you love her *more* and see her the way he does, as his beautiful bride. Jesus bought her with his life. Don't withhold yours from her.

How much do you love the church?

How will you show your love for her?

What can you do for your church today? This week? This month? This year?

---

1. If you are having a hard time finding a gospel-centered church, search the Acts 29 and Gospel Coalition church finder at http://www.acts29network.org/find-churches/ and http://thegospelcoalition.org/network/church-directory/.

May you grow in your love for the body and bride of Christ. May your commitment be greater than ever.

To him be glory in the church and in Christ Jesus throughout all generations, forever and ever. Amen.

EPHESIANS 3:21

CHAPTER 22

Gospel Community Anchors Us to Reality

By the grace given to me I say to everyone among you not to think of himself more highly than he ought to think, but to think with sober judgment, each according to the measure of faith that God has assigned.

ROMANS 12:3

There are two toxic heresies to avoid in life. Both are deadly to your soul. The first is Dumbo's magic feather. Dumbo the elephant can fly, but he doesn't have the confidence or courage to do so without believing in a "magic" feather.

The second deadly heresy is the "Little Engine That Could" mind-set. Remember him? He couldn't get up that hill, but it all changed when he began to say, "I think I can. I think I can. I think I can."

Sadly, this is how many Christians try to get up the hills of the Christian life. The world calls it the power of positive thinking. Phooey! There is no power in positive thinking—not when it comes to kingdom living and matters of eternal consequence. Ultimately there is power only in Jesus. Confidence in life is never found in a mirror but in a risen Savior. Dumbo's feather is just a feather. It's powerless.

We have Christ, the reigning Lord of all things, indwelling our very bodies, and we want to add something to him? Goodness gracious. Reject legalism! Reject all add-ons. We don't need any pink feathers in this life; we have Christ, and he has given us all we need—"His divine power has granted to us all things that pertain to life and godliness, through the knowledge of him who called us to his own glory and excellence" (2 Peter 1:3).

In the gospel, God gives us himself and God gives us each other. The Lord has given us both his Spirit and a Spirit-empowered community. We belong to Christ and we belong to each other. If we are going to grow and mature in Christ, we must reject magic feathers and mere worldly positivism and instead receive help from our brothers and sisters in Christ.

> **In the gospel, God gives us himself and God gives us each other.**

Apollos is an example of one who did. He's one of the best-known, most powerful, and impactful preachers of the gospel in the New Testament. The Corinthians lumped him together with Paul and Peter (1 Cor. 1:12). Luke describes Apollos as eloquent and super-skilled with the Old Testament (Acts 18:24). He'd be a top conference speaker today. But he didn't have his message quite right. When the missionary couple Priscilla and Aquila heard Apollos preach, they realized he was missing something.

So what did they do? "They took him aside and explained to him the way of God more accurately" (Acts 18:26). And Apollos received it. He didn't puff up his chest; he was humble. He didn't say, "Who are you? I'm from Alexandria. I'm brilliant. You are a blue-collar tent maker, and you want to help me with my preaching?" Rather, Apollos gladly received help from his loving brother and sister.

Apollos needed to keep growing—and so do you and I and everyone who reads this book. We all need to keep growing, and we need an environment where other Christians can spur us along. Do you have such a place in your life? If not, look out—a gutter might be around the corner.

I'm a horrible bowler. I've scored a twenty-three before. That's pride-mutilatingly horrible. I would love to use the bumpers every time, but I'm a man. However, I do get to use bumpers when I take my daughter bowling. And when those gorgeous bumpers come up, there are two of them. One won't get it done—I'd just ping-pong into the other gutter. I need both bumpers.

Community and the Bible are the bumpers we need in our lives. The Spirit of Christ uses both to transform us into the image of Christ. The Word of God without a gospel community can be abused, misapplied, and ignored. And a community that isn't centered on the gospel and the Word of God will only gutter itself person by person into nothingness. We need the refining factory of the church of Jesus.

No one has arrived at perfection. Even Paul the apostle, who went to heaven and had conversations with Jesus, said that he still needed to grow:

> In the power of the Spirit, we pull each other back to reality, down from our bigheadedness and fakeness – or up from our condemnation and shame.

Not that I have already obtained this or am already perfect, but I press on to make it my own, because Christ Jesus has made me his own. Brothers, I do not consider that I have made it my own. But one thing I do: forgetting what lies behind and straining forward to what lies ahead, I press on toward the goal for the prize of the upward call of God in Christ Jesus. Let those of us who are mature think this way, and if in anything you think otherwise, God will reveal that also to you. Only let us hold true to what we have attained. (Phil. 3:12–16)

In the power of the Spirit, we pull each other back to reality, down from our bigheadedness and fakeness—or up from our condemnation and shame, reminding each other that we are seated with Christ in the heavenly places (Eph. 2:6). We bring each other back to the gospel realities.

Paul says, "I'm not there yet. I'm not perfect. But I am pressing on into maturity. And that's how mature Christians think." They don't think they need Jesus less; they realize more and more how much they need both him and each other. Do you desire guidance for your life? Habits? Money? Marriage? Do you want encouragement in your evangelism? Do you need correction about your beliefs? What you're looking for can only be found in community with fellow believers.

Our culture sells us on the idea that we can be our own heroes—that we can be the source of the change we want to see in ourselves. Dumbo clutched the feather and people cheered. The Little Engine changed his thinking and got it done. That is unreality. The help you seek is found in a gospel community.

John Owen, one of my favorite brothers from church history, captures the nature of a gospel-centered church. He writes, "A gospel church is a company of faithful professing people, walking together by mutual consent or confederation to the Lord Jesus Christ and one to another, in subjection to and practice of all his gospel precepts and commands, whereby they are separate from all persons and things manifestly contrary or disagreeing thereunto."[1] A gospel church walks together to help each other follow Jesus and move away from all that is contrary to him.

Living in a gospel community takes a lot of wisdom. We are to help each other not with blunt-force words but with words spoken kindly and precisely. Sometimes we deliver needful correction in an unwise fashion—wrong time, wrong place. Wisdom looks to give counsel at the right time and in the right manner. "A word fitly

---

1. John Owen, *The Works of John Owen*, ed. William H. Goold, vol. 16 (Edinburgh: T&T Clark, n.d.), 6.

spoken is like apples of gold in a setting of silver," says Proverbs 25:11. Carefully considered, patient, and precise words along with a humble, nonthreatening tone and posture can get life-shaping results. Priscilla and Aquila pulled Apollos aside and offered their help. Kindness and wisdom won an audience.

> **We are to help each other not with blunt-force words but with words spoken kindly and precisely.**

If you are known as someone who speaks his or her mind, or "tells it like it is," that is not to your honor. "The heart of the righteous ponders how to answer, but the mouth of the wicked pours out evil things" (Prov. 15:28). A hasty tongue isn't humble. It isn't loving. And it won't help your brother or sister for whom Christ died. The goal of gospel-centered communication is to bring grace upon grace. "Let no corrupting talk come out of your mouths, but only such as is good for building up, as fits the occasion, that it may give grace to those who hear" (Eph. 4:29).

Far too many Christians live in a self-induced solitary confinement. That isn't the way of Christ's kingdom. When Jesus died on the cross for our sins, his blood washed over his entire body—the whole church, not just isolated individuals. And when he rose from the dead, we all rose into new life with him. All of us, together. Jesus of Nazareth didn't give his life for an amorphous blob of strangers or loosely affiliated service attenders; he died for his brothers and sisters. The gospel unites us.

"Here there is not Greek and Jew, circumcised and uncircumcised, barbarian, Scythian, slave, free; but Christ is all, and in all" (Col. 3:11). It is in the church of Jesus where we best glorify the Lord—all of our voices in heavenly harmony, exalting the triune God.

"May the God of endurance and encouragement grant you to live in such harmony with one another, in accord with Christ Jesus, that together you may with one voice glorify the God and Father of our Lord Jesus Christ" (Rom. 15:5–6).

May you resolve to not live alone but in the plurality of one voice, glorifying your Lord.

Therefore welcome one another as Christ has
welcomed you, for the glory of God.

Romans 15:7

PART FIVE

What Is
Gospel Mission?

Gospel mission is the call and commitment to spread the good news of the gospel of grace to all kinds of people in all kinds of places.

Gospel mission is the spread of the name and fame of Jesus by gospel proclamation.

CHAPTER 23

We Need Gospel Courage

*Lord . . . grant to your servants to continue
to speak your word with all boldness.*

ACTS 4:29

It has been awhile since I've watched *The Wizard of Oz*. Let's leave Kansas for a second. Dorothy is carried away in a tornado (spoiler alert: she's dreaming), and she meets three companions on her journey to get back home: the Tin Man, the Scarecrow, and the Lion. These characters, sadly, remind me of many Christians, including the one I find in the mirror.

Some Christians are like the Tin Man. They know a lot but relate to others like a cyborg. They don't have any friends, they don't have community, and they don't have a heart for people to meet Jesus.

Other Christians are like the Scarecrow. They mean well—but if they only had a brain! They aren't honed into the Bible. They have a big heart but don't know what the Bible teaches or what God would have for us, and they put more stock in their own word than God's.

And still other Christians are like the Lion—complete cowards in the mission of Christ. They would say, like Peter, "I'll die for you, Lord," but the second an opportunity comes up to speak of our crucified and conquering Christ, they hightail it.

Which one are you most like? Maybe you are a combination.

Fortunately, whichever you gravitate toward, you have a King who makes all of us new. The brave Lion of Judah is conforming us into his image, so we won't be big, 'fraidy cats forever—not with the Spirit of Jesus living within us. Moreover, discipleship grows the Tin Man's heart and helps the Scarecrow think according to Christ and his Word. This is the path of the gospel-formed life: living like Christ, becoming like Christ, and following Christ, by the power of Christ's Spirit.

The gospel is both a call to salvation and a calling on our lives.

The gospel saves. And the gospel sends. Jesus says, "As the Father has sent me, so I am sending you" (John 20:21). The gospel is both a call to salvation and a calling on our lives. We are witnesses (Acts 1:8). And the Lord doesn't leave us to evangelize on our own. He never leaves us. It's his presence that gives us great courage.

The apostle Paul was no cowardly lion. He took beatings and jail time. He even stared down death. Nothing deterred him, because he was convinced of the gospel's magnitude. When Paul was in jail (again), Jesus stood by him and said, "Take courage, for as you have testified to the facts about me in Jerusalem, so you must testify also in Rome" (Acts 23:11). Jesus was communicating two things: he was with Paul, and Paul had more work to do. Paul could have gospel courage because he could trust his Lord.

Paul's story is nothing new. How could Moses march up to Pharaoh and demand the release of God's people? The Lord was with him. How could Joshua march around a city and expect to see walls crumble? The Lord was with him. How could a little shepherd boy kill a decorated enemy warrior who made every Israelite soldier nervous? The Lord was with him.

What about you? How will you talk to your neighbor, family member, or coworker about the gospel of the kingdom? Your Lord is with you. Or taking it even further, why, if called to do so, would you move to a place on earth where the name of Jesus has never been heard? Because he is with you. These are his words: "All authority in heaven and on earth has been given to me. Go therefore and make disciples of all nations, baptizing them in the name of the Father and of the Son and of the Holy Spirit, teaching them to observe all that I have commanded you. And behold, *I am with you always*, to the end of the age" (Matt. 28:18–20, italics mine).

Remember what happened the night Jesus was arrested? His disciples vanished like New Year's resolutions (Matt. 26:56). Remember Peter's meltdown (vv. 69–75)?

Yet a few days later, something monumental happened to the disciples: the risen Jesus met them, and everything changed. A group of pansies were filled with nuclear power.

How did they become so bold? Jesus said, "You will receive power when the Holy Spirit comes upon you" (Acts 1:8 NLT). And that is what happened. In the very next chapter we see Peter—a man who denied Jesus three times out of fear for his own safety—preach the gospel of his risen Lord to thousands. It was a total transformation: a coward became a gospel warrior.

How'd that happen?

> Then Peter, filled with the Holy Spirit, said to them. . . . (Acts 4:8)

See the theme? The Holy Spirit went to work.

Being filled with the Holy Spirit results in wild behavior. The Tin Man in all of us gets a heart of flesh, and our inner Scarecrow receives the mind of Christ. The Spirit moves, not like the spiritual goofiness we see on TV, but like the out-of-the-ordinariness we see in Peter. It's called *power* Holy-Spirit-wrought gospel power. A Spirit-filled believer is a bold gospel-pouring vessel.

One of the glorious gifts of the gospel is the Helper—the Holy Spirit. He helps us "put on the readiness given by the gospel of peace" (Eph. 6:15). The Holy Spirit leads us to say things like, "There is salvation in no one else, for there is no other name under heaven given among men by which we must be saved" (Acts 4:12); and, "We cannot but speak of what we have seen and heard" (v. 20). Spirit-led Christians spread the gospel; the one goes with the other.

If you aren't bold with the gospel, the gospel provides the help you need. Go back to the gospel again. Chew on the gospel more and more. The more the gospel affects you, the more it will invigorate your missional heart for others. Once the gospel is powerful *to* you, it will become powerful *through* you. Giddiness over the gospel will sprout gospel mission. The Bible guarantees it. So if you lack boldness, ask Jesus for it. The gospel grants you the privilege to approach God and ask for the filling of the Spirit.

> Once the gospel is powerful *to* you, it will become powerful *through* you.

In today's verse, the disciples prayed, "Lord, make us bold and keep us bold." If you are a bashful believer, pray that Jesus will make you bold. And if you are already a bold believer, pray that Jesus will make you bolder. Those are the kind of prayers God answers: "And when [the disciples] had prayed, the place in which they were gathered together was shaken, and they were all filled with the Holy Spirit and continued to speak the word of God with boldness" (Acts 4:31).

We could all use some shakin' from the Holy Ghost. Go ask God for it. "How much more will the heavenly Father give the Holy Spirit to those who ask him!" (Luke 11:13).

Will you pray to be filled with more of the Spirit?

Will you pray for boldness?

Will you be bold today?

Who is waiting to hear the gospel from you?

May the God of grace grant you a gospel-readiness that overcomes all of your missional hurdles. May he energize and inspire you to roar with lion-like gospel courage for the fame of his name.

And proclaim as you go, saying, "The kingdom of heaven is at hand."

MATTHEW 10:7

CHAPTER 24

Pointing to the Otherness of Jesus

Therefore, we are ambassadors for Christ, God making his appeal through us. We implore you on behalf of Christ, be reconciled to God. For our sake he made him to be sin who knew no sin, so that in him we might become the righteousness of God.

2 CORINTHIANS 5:20–21

When was the last time you stared at a full moon? I don't mean the last time you glanced at the moon across your driveway while darting from your car to your house to watch a Blu-ray. I mean, when was the last time you stopped in your tracks and gawked at the moon in all its fullness? It's astounding.

Like me, my daughter has been captivated by the wonder of the full moon. One night, on our drive home after a great time eating with friends, my family and I were watching the full moon through our windshield. We were all locked on—especially Ivy. A three-year-old experiences an unfiltered enjoyment of that magnificent, glowing disc hanging in the night sky.

Ivy yelled, "Guys! The moon! It's huge! Look at it!"

I responded, "Yes, Ivy. It's incredible. Jesus made that moon! Amazing, huh?"

Then my little girl said something as brilliant as anything I've heard from any scientist or NASA engineer (or anyone who has played one in the movies): "The moon is so sunny."

The moon is sunny? I had to stop myself from correcting her—because she's totally right. The moon *is* sunny. The moon has no light of its own; it is a giant reflector. The only light the moon has is the Sun's light—and that's the moon's purpose, to reflect the light of the Sun.

The moon is our model. Evangelism isn't about us; we are here to point to the sunniness—to the eye-opening, sin-blinding brilliance—of Jesus, who said, "I am the light of the world." His light is our light; because of him, we ourselves shine in a way that glorifies God. In Jesus' words, "You are the light of the world. A city set on a hill cannot be hidden. Nor do people light a lamp and put it under a basket, but on a stand, and it gives light to all in the house. In the same way, let your light shine before others, so that they may see your good works and give glory to your Father who is in heaven" (Matt. 5:14–16).

In the theological solar system, Jesus is the sun and we are the moon. We are reflectors. Our mission in evangelism is to humbly proclaim the radiant otherness of Jesus, not ourselves. This is the very essence of being Christlike. As John the Baptist said, "He must increase, I must decrease." Tragically, many pastors, authors, churches, and individual Christians have eclipsed the glory of the gospel with goofiness in our churches and ungodly attitudes toward the culture. It's time to get back to what is of first importance.

> In the theological solar system, Jesus is the sun and we are the moon. We are reflectors.

Evangelism is squarely about a cross and a tomb, not our pet agendas, social issues, or political opinions. Reflecting the Sun—that's the moon's job. And our glorious task, empowered by the Spirit of Jesus, is to point to the Son, to reflect the Light of the World. Paul reminds us:

> Therefore, having this ministry by the mercy of God, we do not lose heart. But we have renounced

disgraceful, underhanded ways. We refuse to practice cunning or to tamper with God's word, but by the open statement of the truth we would commend ourselves to everyone's conscience in the sight of God. And even if our gospel is veiled, it is veiled to those who are perishing. In their case the god of this world has blinded the minds of the unbelievers, to keep them from seeing the light of the gospel of the glory of Christ, who is the image of God. For what we proclaim is not ourselves, but Jesus Christ as Lord, with ourselves as your servants for Jesus' sake. For God, who said, "Let light shine out of darkness," has shone in our hearts to give the light of the knowledge of the glory of God in the face of Jesus Christ. (2 Cor. 4:1–6)

The apostle Paul didn't grow up in the church. He was its persecutor; he hated the church. Paul wasn't the criminal type; he was the intellectual, moral, religious type. And he couldn't stand Jesus of Nazareth or his followers—until he came face-to-face with the postcrucifixion, resurrected, once again breathing Jesus. His encounter changed everything. It changed the world—and it changes our evangelism.

As Paul says, we do not proclaim ourselves. We announce a bright and shining gospel. It is time for us to dust off our ancient gospel, renounce any sleight of hand, bait-and-switch, razzmatazz evangelism strategies, and simply do what the apostles did: point to the otherness of the Lord Jesus.

We are here to proclaim that a man from the first century still reigns as the King of kings twenty centuries later, and he invites all people to believe in him. Do you feel the oddity of that statement? How strange the gospel must sound to the world! In the words of

Southern Baptist ethicist Russell Moore, "The power of the Gospel is found in the freakishness of the Gospel."[1]

Think about how against the grain Jesus is. There is no one else like him—so great, so kind, so inviting, so awesome. He is far more important and incredible than, and radically different from, anyone else who has ever put his or her feet on the earth. Either this Galilean son of a carpenter is the Son of God, or he should be stamped as a freak and forgotten. He is either the long-expected Messiah-King of the Hebrew Scriptures, or he is cut from the same looney-bin cloth as Charles Manson, David Koresh—shoot, even Lady Gaga.

> We are here to proclaim that a man from the first century still reigns as the King of kings twenty centuries later.

As C.S. Lewis says, "Socrates did not claim to be Zeus, nor the Buddha to be Bramah, nor Mohammed to be Allah. That sort of claim occurs only in Our Lord and in admitted quacks or lunatics. I agree that we don't 'demand crystal perfection in other men,' nor do we find it. But if there is one Man in whom we do find it, and if that one Man also claims to be more than man, what then?"[2]

The *what* is worship. Jesus is to be worshiped. He is to be followed. There is no middle way. If Jesus isn't the King of kings—well, then, he's vile, the most disgusting person ever to walk this planet, or he is off his rocker. I mean, think about some of the things Jesus said. They are audacious.

> *He said he came from heaven.* "I have come down from heaven, not to do my own will but the will of him who sent me." (John 6:38)

---

1. Tom Strode, "Moore: Church Returning to Oddness in Culture," *Baptist Press*, September 18, 2013, http://www.bpnews.net/bpnews.asp?ID=41114.

2. C.S. Lewis, *The Collected Letters of C.S. Lewis*, vol. 3 (New York: HarperCollins, 2007), 1377–78.

He said he existed before Abraham. "Your father Abraham rejoiced that he would see my day. He saw it and was glad." So the Jews said to him, "You are not yet fifty years old, and have you seen Abraham?" Jesus said to them, "Truly, truly, I say to you, before Abraham was, I am." (John 8:56–58)

He said he would die and then rise. "The Son of Man must suffer many things and be rejected by the elders and chief priests and scribes, and be killed, and on the third day be raised." (Luke 9:22)

He claims to be the Galactic Emperor. Jesus came and said to them, "All authority in heaven and on earth has been given to me." (Matt. 28:18)

He said the Old Testament is all about him. "You search the Scriptures because you think that in them you have eternal life; and it is they that bear witness about me." (John 5:39)

What kind of man says stuff like this and is revered for two millennia? What if I said those things? You'd think I was a psycho, more fit for living on the subway than in the suburbs. But Jesus isn't kidding around and he isn't a psycho-freakazoid. He is no mere man; he is the God-man. He is very God of very God. He is the eternal Son of God. Jesus of Nazareth is no insignificant Middle Easterner. He really is God, the Emperor of the Cosmos, who laid down his life as a ransom for many, dying a traitor's death to save sinners like you and me (Matt. 20:28).

> **A crucified champion: That is totally other than the world's idea of victory.**

A crucified champion: That is totally

other than the world's idea of victory and what many so-called ministry experts think appeals to our culture. But that didn't bother the apostle Paul. He wrote, "We preach Christ crucified, a stumbling block to Jews and folly to Gentiles, but to those who are called, both Jews and Greeks, Christ the power of God and the wisdom of God. For the foolishness of God is wiser than men, and the weakness of God is stronger than men" (1 Cor. 1:23–25).

C.S. Lewis helps us out again: "The doctrine of Christ's divinity seems to me not something stuck on which you can unstick but something that peeps out at every point so that you'd have to unravel the whole web to get rid of it."[3] The importance of Jesus' Godness cannot be overemphasized, and it certainly cannot be over-rejoiced in. Only the real Jesus gives us real joy.

Hardly anyone thinks Jesus was a bad guy. But far too many people think Jesus was simply a "good guy." We must remember that there is no *was* with Jesus—Jesus *is*. Jesus is alive, and he is far too extreme to let us keep the good-guy sugarcoat on him. To do so is to ignore not just his teachings but also his claims about himself. That's dishonest. Jesus won't let us maintain any fairy tale about him being anything less than God and Savior. He defies our attempts to merely "respect" him and dismiss him. He demands worship. He calls for you and me to entrust our lives to him.

> The real Jesus – the one we find in the gospels and in the letters of the New Testament – induces way more than yawns. He ignites awe.

That's the Jesus we have to deal with. He won't be ignored. Many people aren't interested in Jesus because the one who is presented to them is, quite frankly, uninteresting. But the real Jesus—the one we find in the gospels and in the letters

---

3. Ibid., 1555.

of the New Testament—induces way more than yawns. He ignites awe.

Are you with him? The Son of God died for sins and rose again to forgive us, to declare us clean, and to give us new life. He's far more than a good public speaker, far greater than Tony Robbins at his best. He is our Life and our Light, the Sun to our moon. And *that* is why we proclaim not ourselves, nor do we announce some cute and cuddly Christ. We have a big, mighty, lofty, kind, and magnificent Jesus to tell the world about. His light shines through us. We don't hide it under the basket of a Jesus who is too safe.

May you let him shine. Evangelism is about pointing to the otherness of Jesus. He's way more captivating than a full moon.

How precious is your steadfast love, O God!
The children of mankind take refuge in the shadow of your wings.
They feast on the abundance of your house,
and you give them drink from the river of your delights.
For with you is the fountain of life;
in your light do we see light.

PSALM 36:7–9

CHAPTER 25

The Gospel Mobilizes Us for Mission

You are a chosen race, a royal priesthood, a holy nation, a people for his own possession, that you may proclaim the excellencies of him who called you out of darkness into his marvelous light.

1 PETER 2:9

I don't know where your soda allegiances lie, but we all draw the line somewhere. I'm not a complicated guy, but I have standards. When at a restaurant and I ask the server for a Coke Zero, nothing irks my soul more in that moment, maybe even in that week, than to hear, "Will Diet Pepsi work?" I have to bite my tongue every time. I want to reply, "Will Monopoly money work?"

I can't stand Pepsi, let alone Diet Pepsi. Good grief! I thought we were an advanced society!

But as bad as I personally find Diet Pepsi to be,[1] I can think of something worse: a *hot* Diet Pepsi. Picture an open can roasting in your car during summer. Take a sip. Disgusting, right? There are few things on this planet less exciting than a hot, flat Diet Pepsi. One of them is the kind of life that many Christians have settled for.

---

1. If you like Diet Pepsi, that's OK, I'll still be your friend. I hope you come around to Coke Zero. There's room for you in my Diet Soda Denomination.

I'm convinced that many of us sit yawning in the kingdom of God because we aren't living as kingdom dwellers. We are more like the world than we'd dare admit. We are unlike Father Abraham, who "was looking forward to the city that has foundations, whose designer and builder is God" (Heb. 11:10). The things of earth haven't grown as strangely dim as we'd like. And typically, our Christian experience sags.

There is a remedy for our mediocrity: the Holy Spirit.

Acts 1:8 is in the Bible to show us what is possible with the Spirit of Christ. When the Holy Spirit shows up, no matter where you turn in the Scriptures, pyrotechnics follow, either internally or externally. When the Holy Spirit came upon the apostles, they acquired exactly what Jesus promised: power—tangible, salty, bright, world-changing power. Not power to break walls of ice, rip phone books in half, or other circus shenanigans, but power with a gospel purpose. "You will receive power when the Holy Spirit has come upon you," Jesus said, "and *you will be my witnesses* in Jerusalem and in all Judea and Samaria, and to the end of the earth" (Acts 1:8, italics mine).

> When the Holy Spirit shows up, no matter where you turn in the Scriptures, pyrotechnics follow.

The power is for proclamation; the Spirit of Christ is for the spreading of the name of Christ. When the Spirit lands, he arms us with supernatural resources and sends us on a mission: to call people's gaze to a bloody cross and a vacant tomb. This power is fearless, bold. It keeps us swinging our swords for the kingdom cause of making disciples.

So if we aren't experiencing the atomic power of the Spirit, perhaps it's because we aren't doing the things that require him to show up. We aren't retelling the dead-raising truth of God in the flesh pouring out his blood, coming back to life, saving sinners, and offering new life and forgiveness to all who will look to him. Evangelism invites the lost to Jesus, and it also draws us back to Jesus; we behold him afresh. The power of the Spirit is for us to be witnesses to the death and resurrection of Jesus Christ.

Here's what we must do: We have to give up on the lesser power of self. We cannot run for long on the fumes of self-importance, self-will, or self-protection. A daily crucifixion of self and a daily reunion with the Lord Jesus reminds us of our identity and activity as followers of the Way. We are witnesses. We cannot say, "It's all about Jesus" and not witness to the facts of what happened one weekend in Jerusalem two thousand years ago.

Jesus said, "You will be my witnesses." That's significant. We are *his* witnesses. We belong to him. He's given us a holy task and he's given us his Holy Spirit.

> He's given us a holy task and he's given us his Holy Spirit.

You and I exist to make much of Jesus, to testify about our risen Lord. The Holy Spirit wants to make disciples and magnify Jesus, and he works in us and through us to make him famous. Discipleship is much more than helping Christians make moral and sanitized decisions in life; it's also about stewarding the gospel and passing on the mission to the next generation.

Discipleship is for disciple making. It might start with your humbly seeking discipleship in gospel community. Or it might be time for you to shake off the dust and begin the process of showing others how to live for Christ in all of life. Gospel mission spreads through the patient discipleship of ordinary Christians.

Our confidence in the progress of the gospel and the kingdom of God doesn't depend on bookstores, politicians, Christian athletes, or pop icons. It has nothing to do with evangelicalism's popularity in the culture, with pastors zip-lining to the stage, or with the next big religious fad to reach the world. Spare me! Our assurance is in the power of the Holy Spirit. He makes revival happen, he plants churches, he raises up leaders, and he causes sinners to be born again. Without the Spirit, there would be no Bible, no preachers, no conversions, no worldwide mission, no disciple making. It is the Holy Spirit who takes fishermen and turns them into world-flipping, missional monsters—and that same Spirit is in *you*.

The Spirit may be invisible, but he is humongous. The Spirit of God doesn't work in just a corner of your life—he wants to fill it! Does he work in droplets? No. *Gushes.* How else did Paul go from persecuting Christ's church to pleading with people to believe in Jesus? How else did a group of 120 men and women from the Middle East spread Jesus' name to every livable continent? We have a Spirit of power.

> We don't need to know a lot, but we do need to know one thing to be witnesses: the glorious gospel of grace.

Gospel mission isn't dependent on our ability. This realization should defuse our fears and hang-ups about proclaiming Jesus' name. We don't need to know a lot, but we do need to know one thing to be witnesses: the glorious gospel of grace. Cherish Christ, trust Christ, and the Spirit of Christ will lead you through the thickets and thorns of evangelism to its joyous harvest.

In his book, *Gospel Deeps*, Jared Wilson nails it:

> I am not an expert in missiology or ecclesiology or sociology, but I can read what the Bible says. In its pages I read that the source of the church's power is the Holy Spirit working through the proclamation of the gospel of Jesus Christ. No other source is credited with transforming power, not even intelligence or good works, much less creativity and good marketing. Uneducated men with stuttering tongues and unclever speech set the world on fire because they

were content to simply arrange the wood and trust the torch of the gospel to do its thing.[2]

The Lord isn't looking for eloquent speech givers; he's looking for simple folk who will walk by faith. The gospel is enough. Jesus wants to use ordinary you and me for his extraordinary purposes. The more soaked we are in his glorious gospel, his wonder-working power, the more it will seep out of the pores of our lives. "The Holy Spirit takes the fool, and makes him know the wonders of redeeming love," says Charles Spurgeon.[3] Hallelujah! Sign me up.

What do we need for gospel mission? How do we escape the Diet Pepsiness of our lives? The wonders of redeeming love—found in the Bible and lived in the church by the power of the Spirit—is the key. Why not pray for that today?

May the Spirit of Christ show you the wonders of the Redeemer's love, moving you further in a faithful life of mission.

———————

If I preach the gospel, that gives me no ground
for boasting. For necessity is laid upon me.
Woe to me if I do not preach the gospel!

1 Corinthians 9:16

———————

2. Jared C. Wilson, *Gospel Deeps: Reveling in the Excellencies of Jesus* (Wheaton, IL: Crossway, 2012), 45.

3. C.H. Spurgeon, *The Metropolitan Tabernacle Pulpit Sermons*, vol. 39 (London: Passmore & Alabaster, 1883), 497.

CHAPTER 26

Welcome to the Mission Field

I am not ashamed of the gospel, for it is the power
of God for salvation to everyone who believes,
to the Jew first and also to the Greek.

ROMANS 1:16

If Jesus saved you, then Jesus also put you on his mission. Jesus says he "came to seek and to save the lost" (Luke 19:10). And now he tells us, "Peace be with you. As the Father has sent me, even so I am sending you" (John 20:21). Without any rocket-science methods of interpreting these verses, we see that we are sent like Jesus, by Jesus, to seek and save the lost. That's the mission.

How faithful are you to the mission? How faithful are you being to the One who sent you? I'm not talking about selling your house, your goodies, and moving to Zimbabwe. Being on mission doesn't necessarily mean relocating. It might, but mission unfolds wherever you are. Gospel mission rearranges your thinking: "In light of God's providence, I am a missionary wherever I go."

We are always entering the mission field. As with Paul in Athens, waiting is never just waiting.[1] God can use what we think to

---

1. "While Paul was waiting for them at Athens, his spirit was provoked within him as he saw that the city was full of idols. So he reasoned in the synagogue with the Jews and the devout persons, and in the marketplace every day with those who happened to be there" (Acts 17:16–17).

be empty moments, maybe even derailed moments, for his glory. Look and listen for opportunities to talk about Jesus. Cab rides, grocery store checkout lines, soccer practices, mailboxes, salons and barbershops—all are ripe soil for evangelism.

> God can use what we think to be empty moments, maybe even derailed moments, for his glory.

What would happen if Jesus told you *not* to go on a mission trip? Do you have a grid for that?

Consider the demon-possessed man in the eighth chapter of Luke. This guy lived in a cemetery, broke the iron chains used to restrain him as if they were confetti, and ran around naked. He was filled with so many demons, he would have made the girl in *The Exorcist* nervous. In fact, the demons gave their collective name as Legion.

And then Jesus showed up. The man fell down on his knees before him—and then, suddenly, he was Legion-free. At a word from Jesus, the demons left the man and inhabited a herd of pigs (Luke 8:33). When the townspeople arrived a while later to check things out, they found the man in his right mind, clothed (praise the Lord), and sitting with Jesus.

But the story doesn't end there. Luke continues, "The man from whom the demons had gone begged that he might be with him, but Jesus sent him away, saying, 'Return to your home, and declare how much God has done for you.' And he went away, proclaiming throughout the whole city how much Jesus had done for him" (vv. 38–39).

Think about that. The man begged to go on mission with Jesus. Pleaded. And Jesus said no. Shocking, isn't it? The guy had a killer testimony. He probably had a heart for those who were oppressed by demons, and he wanted to minister to them. But when he applied for the trip, he got turned down. Jesus didn't want him to head off on a mission trip—Jesus wanted him to remain at home. Because the man's mission field was right where he lived. He didn't need to travel around with Jesus; he could proclaim the kingdom of God right on his block. And that's exactly what he did. He went throughout his entire city and told them about the power of Christ in his life.

Has your whole family heard? Do the people close by you know what God has done for you? If you believe the Holy Spirit is calling you to other parts of the world, that's great. There are 7,000 unreached people groups in the world today. We need people to go to them. Maybe that's you—may God raise up many people to go to the nations! And we also need people proclaiming Jesus in their own towns and in their everyday lives. One place is not more important than the other; overseas and across the street both need the good news of the kingdom of God. Honduras, Thailand, Kenya, Oklahoma City, New Orleans, London, and Tomball, Texas—all need missionaries.

> One place is not more important than the other; overseas and across the street both need the good news of the kingdom of God.

Mission trips can be a good and godly thing. Some trips can also be a complete waste of money, nothing more than a baptized vacation. Not all mission trips are created equal. But that's not the point. The *desire* to serve Christ, whether overseas, underground, or downtown, is a holy thing. Think, however, about who you are and where you live. Are you living a gospel-centered life *here*? Maybe you don't need to journey abroad. Maybe you just need to realize you're already on the mission field right where you are.

Evangelism isn't a mystical experience—it's normal. Evangelism happens every day. It's like talking about a delicious meal or a restaurant: you simply share the pleasure of your experience. Missional living is telling others about the gospeliciousness you've discovered and inviting them to the table.

You might feel weak, scared, worried, or nearly paralyzed about sharing the gospel. Before you believe your feelings, believe that you are filled with the Holy Spirit and he is rumbling inside you with the power of the risen Jesus to share the gospel. You are filled with so much power from the Spirit of God that it makes a Category 5 hurricane jealous. The Hulk wears Holy Spirit pajamas. Trust the Spirit, not yourself, in your evangelism.

> You aren't some Bible-thumper; you are an ambassador for Christ, a proclaimer of excellencies, a bright hilltop city.

You aren't some Bible-thumper; you are an ambassador for Christ, a proclaimer of excellencies, a bright hilltop city.[2] Gospel-centered evangelism does not get bogged down with peripheral issues like literary criticism, day-age theory, or pre-/mid-/post-trib yada yada. These all have their place, but gospel-centered evangelism focuses on the focal point: the person and work of Jesus Christ. Don't be an evangelist for anything but the evangel—that is, the gospel.

May you not be ashamed of the gospel. May you believe it truly

---

2. *Ambassadors*: "Therefore, we are ambassadors for Christ, God making his appeal through us. We implore you on behalf of Christ, be reconciled to God" (2 Cor. 5:20–21). *Christ's excellencies*: "You are a chosen race, a royal priesthood, a holy nation, a people for his own possession, that you may proclaim the excellencies of him who called you out of darkness into his marvelous light. Once you were not a people, but now you are God's people; once you had not received mercy, but now you have received mercy" (1 Peter 2:9–10). *Hilltop city*: "Nor do people light a lamp and put it under a basket, but on a stand, and it gives light to all in the house. In the same way, let your light shine before others, so that they may see your good works and give glory to your Father who is in heaven" (Matt. 5:15–16).

is the power of God unto salvation. May you brag on your Lord.
Boast in him, for he is great. Grand. Worthy.

———————————

The love of Christ controls us,
because we have concluded this: that one has died for all,
therefore all have died; and he died for all,
that those who live might no longer live for themselves
but for him who for their sake died and was raised.

2 Corinthians 5:14–15

CHAPTER 27

Gospel Enjoyment Leads to Gospel Mission

Oh, magnify the LORD with me,
and let us exalt his name together! . . .
Oh, taste and see that the LORD is good!

PSALM 34:3, 8

Imagine that you discovered the best chocolate cake you've ever tasted at a local hole-in-the-wall. Naturally, you begin to tell friends and strangers where they can find this masterpiece. They can hear the excitement and urgency in your voice: "You have to go there, for real! It's crazy good." Not hard to imagine, right?

The church word for that story is *evangelism*. We can be enthused evangelists for sports, music, movies, and food—so why do we stall out when it comes to the evangel, the gospel? It's chocolate cake, not chopped liver. It's motivated not by duty, guilt, or churchiness but by sheer enjoyment. In Psalm 34, King David not only proclaims the goodness of God, but he also invites others *into* the goodness of God. "Let's exalt his name together!" David says. "Taste and see that God is good. I have!"

Evangelism is cooked in the oven of enjoyment. Gospel mission grows out of gospel enjoyment. Lack of enjoying God and the gospel breeds groggy evangelism and a mission that's as exciting as an empty fish bowl. We lose our gladness over the gospel

> Gospel mission grows out of gospel enjoyment.

when we forget the flavor of forgiveness, and then we no longer see the gospel as the powerful news for today, but only as grace for yesterday. The gospel is joyous news for yesterday, today, and tomorrow—and eternity. When the gospel recedes to the margin of our lives, it's no surprise that mission and evangelism become unimportant.

But there is good news. Lack of mission can be remedied by finding your joy again. Re-taste and re-see that the Lord is good to scoundrels like you and me. Go back to the glory of the gospel.

Evangelism isn't the church's version of Avon. We aren't selling cosmetics, or vacuum cleaners, or anything, for that matter, and we aren't peddling some first century relic. Evangelism is joy on overflow. Gospel mission is inviting the downcast to the fountain of delight—to God himself. Gospel mission is more than swaying people from eternal damnation: it's inviting them to the table of glory where the God of the gospel can satisfy their souls.

> **Once you are thrilled with the gospel, mission won't have to be forced – it will spill out of you.**

Gospel-centeredness is a serious commitment to be in awe of the gospel. It's a resolve to drink—to gulp!—from the joy hydrant. Being centered on the good news means having it always before our souls, remembering our great God and Savior, seeing the bloody tree and the empty tomb, rejoicing over forgiveness and freedom, and living a new life by the life and death of Jesus in our place. The gospel-centered Christian sings,

> Prone to wander, Lord, I feel it.
> Prone to leave the God I love.
> Here's my heart, Lord. Take and seal it.
> Seal it for thy courts above. (Robert Robinson,
>   "Come Thou Fount of Every Blessing," 1757)

Enjoy gospel truth today. Sit in it. Meditate on it for hours if you need to. Once you are thrilled with the gospel, mission won't have to be forced—it will spill out of you. Gospel on the heart equals gospel on the tongue. The more your heart resounds with

> Glory! Glory! This I sing—
> Nothing but the blood of Jesus;
> All my praise for this I bring—
> Nothing but the blood of Jesus. (Robert Lowry,
>   "Nothing but the Blood of Jesus," 1876)

the more supernaturally natural evangelism will become for you.

May you enjoy the gospel today. May you drink deep from the sweet cup of grace. May gospel mission be your natural response to the feast of gospel enjoyment. Taste and see—and pull out a chair for someone else.

But let all who take refuge in you rejoice;
let them ever sing for joy, and spread your protection over them,
that those who love your name may exult in you.

PSALM 5:11

Keep Going

*Finally, then, brothers, we ask and urge you in
the Lord Jesus, that as you received from us how
you ought to walk and to please God, just as you
are doing, that you do so more and more.*

1 THESSALONIANS 4:1

Today is our last reading. This book is finished, but the journey isn't.
Gospel formation is more than a destination. It's a mobile fortress—
one where you must fight idols, slay legalistic opponents that live in
your heart, and keep loving the Lord your God with all your heart,
soul, mind, strength, intelligence, schedule, passions, debit cards,
gifts, possessions, and family—all because you've made it your aim
to please Jesus.[1] Jesus is your message, your model, your motivation,
and the means to glorifying God in all you do.

When we begin to think with a gospel-centered heart, we realize
that gospel-centeredness is an "already but not yet." We have to keep
going *there*. We've walked into the room, and now we keep walking—further up, further in, deeper and deeper into the fountain of
glory. And the further we go, the harder it is to go back to legalism,
gospel-boredom, lukewarmness, and the sins we used to hold so dear.

Pursue gospel-centeredness—pursue Jesus—just as you are doing, more and more. Don't stop. Paul didn't—and he caught a pre-
view of heaven.

---

1. "Whether we are at home or away, we make it our aim to please him"
(2 Cor. 5:9).

> Not that I have already obtained this or am already
> perfect, but I press on to make it my own, because
> Christ Jesus has made me his own. Brothers, I do not
> consider that I have made it my own. But one thing I
> do: forgetting what lies behind and straining forward
> to what lies ahead, I press on toward the goal for the
> prize of the upward call of God in Christ Jesus. Let
> those of us who are mature think this way, and if in
> anything you think otherwise, God will reveal that
> also to you. (Phil. 3:12–15)

The good news is that God can do this work in your heart—and he will. That's good news, because we couldn't even come close to gospel-centeredness on our own. We can't travel through the fields of glory without our owner and keeper, the author and perfecter of our faith. We don't know the way, but like the shepherd of Psalm 23, he'll shepherd us through.[2]

My final prayer for you is not original; I've hijacked it from Paul's second letter to the church in Thessalonica: "May the Lord direct your hearts to the love of God and to the steadfastness of Christ" (2 Thess. 3:5).

Let's take that one element at a time.

May the Lord direct your hearts. He, and only he, can do this. Let's ask him to move our hearts toward experiencing, to an ever-increasing degree, two life-changing realities . . .

The love of God. This is no junior high love—it's divine, the greatest love, supernatural love. The Cosmic King has shown you love. Behold his bloodstained love, fixed on nails to save his enemies and

---

2. "I am the good shepherd. I know my own and my own know me, just as the Father knows me and I know the Father; and I lay down my life for the sheep. And I have other sheep that are not of this fold. I must bring them also, and they will listen to my voice. So there will be one flock, one shepherd" (John 10:14–16).

make them his friends. Your God's love for you is beyond anything you can comprehend—he is omni-loving.

The steadfastness of Christ. Jesus is with you. He's unshakable. He's never been flustered. So don't worry. He will never leave you hanging. His commitment to you is stronger than a ten-thousand-foot-thick concrete wall. His shepherd's arm is with you all the way. Today when you sin, and tomorrow when you sin bigger, Christ is bigger still. On Christ the solid rock you stand; all other ground is sinking sand.

Charles Spurgeon, preaching on 2 Thessalonians 3:5, invites us to see the bountiful love of God, saying:

> If we further enter into the love of God, we see its immeasurable greatness. There is a little word which you have often heard, which I beg to bring before you again—that little word "so." "God *so* loved the world that he gave his only begotten Son, that whosoever believeth in him should not perish, but have everlasting life." Come, ye surveyors, bring your chains, and try to make a survey of this word "so." Nay, that is not enough. Come hither, ye that make our national surveys, and lay down charts for all nations. Come, ye who map the sea and land, and make a chart of this word "so." Nay, I must go further. Come hither, ye astronomers, that with your optic glasses spy out spaces before which imagination staggers, come hither and encounter calculations worthy of all your powers! When you have measured between the horns of space, here is a task that will defy you—"God *so* loved the world." If you enter into *that*, you will know that all this love is to you—that while Jehovah loves the world, yet he loves you as much as if there were

nobody else in all the world to love. God can pour the
infinite love of his heart upon one object, and yet, for
all that, can love ten thousand times ten thousand of
his creatures just as much. O heir of God, thy store of
love is not diminished because the innumerable company of thy brethren share it with thee! Thy Father
loves each child as well as if he had no other. Peer into
this abyss of love. Plunge into this sea. Dive into this
depth unsearchable. Oh, that God might direct you
into the immeasurable greatness of this love![3]

Keep looking to Jesus: this is gospel-centeredness. Keep it all
about Jesus. A grace-addicted, truth-filled, Jesus-exalting life is the
aim of the gospel. Let's chase that goal. Let's ask God to rend the
heavens and visit us with this kind of life. He can do it.

May the Lord do this work in our hearts. May he direct our gaze
to the unwavering love of God and the unbreakable steadfastness
of Christ.

---

*Make every effort to supplement your faith with virtue,
and virtue with knowledge, and knowledge with
self-control, and self-control with steadfastness, and
steadfastness with godliness, and godliness with brotherly
affection, and brotherly affection with love. For if these
qualities are yours and are increasing, they keep you
from being ineffective or unfruitful in the knowledge
of our Lord Jesus Christ. . . . Therefore, brothers, be all
the more diligent to confirm your calling and election,
for if you practice these qualities you will never fall.*

2 PETER 1:5–8, 10

---

3. C.H. Spurgeon, *The Metropolitan Tabernacle Pulpit Sermons*, vol. 34 (London: Passmore & Alabaster, 1883), 328–29.